S/12
K

13x 17 (12)
OP21

DICKENS'S
VICTORIAN LONDON

DICKENS'S
VICTORIAN LONDON

1839–1901

ALEX WERNER

AND

TONY WILLIAMS

MUSEUM OF LONDON

EBURY PRESS

1 3 5 7 9 10 8 6 4 2

First published in 2011 by Ebury Press,
an imprint of Ebury Publishing

A Random House Group Company

The Random House Group Limited Reg. No. 954009

Addresses for companies within the Random House Group can be found at www.randomhouse.co.uk

A CIP catalogue record for this book is available from the British Library

MAY 1 1 2012 _LBI_

The Random House Group Limited supports The Forest Stewardship Council (FSC®),
the leading international forest certification organisation. Our books carrying the FSC label are
printed on FSC® certified paper. FSC is the only forest certification scheme endorsed by the
leading environmental organisations, including Greenpeace. Our paper procurement
policy can be found at www.randomhouse.co.uk/environment

To buy books by your favourite authors and register for offers visit www.randomhouse.co.uk

Endpapers: Stanford's library map of London and its suburbs, 1862 (details from sheets 10 and 11)
Half-title page: St Mary Overy's Dock, Southwark, 1881
Title page: Westminster Abbey and the Palace of Westmister, 1857

Designed by Peter Ward

Printed and bound in Germany by Firmengruppe APPL, aprinta druck, Wemding

ISBN 9780091943738

CONTENTS

INTRODUCTION

'What an amazing place London was to me when I saw it in the distance, and how I believed all the adventures of all my favourite heroes to be constantly enacting and re-enacting there . . . I made it out in my own mind to be fuller of wonders and wickedness than all the cities of the earth . . .'

David Copperfield's initial reaction to London in Charles Dickens's 1849 novel paints a picture of a wondrous, enticing metropolis promising a world of possibilities to the young boy. The magnet that is our capital city has always provided unlimited scope for the imagination, and few observers or writers took so much advantage of that as did Dickens.

For Copperfield, however, the city became a place of suffering, first at school at Salem House, and later when he is sent to work at Murdstone and Grinby's wine business, washing and labelling bottles: a thinly-disguised account, though no one knew it at the time, of Dickens's own childhood sufferings pasting labels at a blacking factory shortly after his arrival in London. The factory where Dickens worked was initially near the river at Hungerford Stairs (see page 11), just as Copperfield describes Murdstone and Grinby's Blackfriars building, 'A crazy old house with a wharf of its own, abutting on the water when the tide was in, and on the mud when the tide was out, and literally overrun with rats.'

Dickens's word-pictures of London did not simply describe a backdrop, a stage set, upon which the novelist's artfully-drawn characters would play out their lives, loves, hates and fears. London itself is a central presence in the novels, a character in its own right. The early photographic pioneers – and when Dickens penned *David Copperfield* the new art form was very much in its infancy – may have found difficulties in capturing the landmarks and streetlife

Left: Cheapside, 1823, W Duryer and T M Baynes

of a grimy, mid-nineteenth century London. But the novelist's detailed, pin-sharp recollections of places and characters, of sounds, smells and sights, help to bring to life a London that would otherwise be all but lost to us.

To speak of Dickens's London as if it was one constant thing is, of course, misleading. During his lifetime – not a long one, for he died in 1870 at the relatively young age of fifty-eight – Dickens shared the experience of all those born in the early years of the nineteenth century; he lived through decades of sweeping change in the city's size, fabric and social structure. Dickens was twenty-five years old when Victoria became Queen on 20 June 1837 and the age became known as Victorian. His childhood and early adult life were spent in Georgian and Regency London and it is this world upon which he draws for his novels. Dickens was alive to the fast-moving changes which were going on all around him, and when we read his works we witness the growth and development of the modern city, with all its associated problems. His descriptions evoke a lost world for us, in the same way that contemporary photographs provide us with a visual record of the city that he knew and which has changed so markedly since his time. It is that world which the photographs in this volume recreate for us, two hundred years since Dickens was born.

Like several of his best-known characters, Dickens was not a native Londoner, but one of the masses whose families moved to the growing metropolis for work. Charles John Huffam Dickens was born

General Coach Office
CROSS KEYS INN,
WOOD STREET. CHEAPSIDE.

Wm. HORNE, Proprietor.

on 7 February 1812, in Portsmouth, where his father John worked as a clerk in the Navy Pay Office at the Royal Dockyard. He came to London as a ten-year-old child in September 1822, when his father's job was transferred from the navy's office in Chatham, Kent, to its headquarters at Somerset House on the Strand. For the rest of Dickens's life, the city would be his muse.

Dickens describes his arrival from Chatham (which he renamed Dullborough) in one of his *The Uncommercial Traveller* essays which appeared in his weekly journal, *All the Year Round*, in June 1860,

'As I left Dullborough in the days when there were no railroads in the land, I left it in a stage-coach. Through all the years that have since passed, have I ever lost the smell of the damp straw in which I was packed – like game – and forwarded, carriage paid, to the Cross Keys, Wood-street, Cheapside, London? There was no other inside passenger, and I consumed my sandwiches in solitude and dreariness, and it rained hard all the way . . .'

The coach journey from Kent to London would have taken about five hours and after crossing the Thames at London Bridge, ended at The Cross Keys in Wood Street, one of London's former coaching inns (demolished in 1865), just off Cheapside (see timetable, left).

The Dickens family had moved to the city in June, but young Charles had remained behind in order to complete his current term's education at William Giles's school in Chatham. Although John Dickens and his family, including the three-year-old Charles, had lived briefly in London in 1815, the period of their more significant residence in the metropolis dates from John Dickens's return to Somerset House. The family moved in to 16 Bayham Street in Camden Town. Properties like those on Bayham Street, some three miles north of the centre of the city, had been built about ten years before, when Camden was still a rural area. This changed during the 1820s and 1830s as the burgeoning city began to sprawl outwards to encroach on the surrounding farms and fields (see Cruikshank illustration, page 13). The new suburb was criss-crossed with the developing canal system

Coach timetable, c.1830

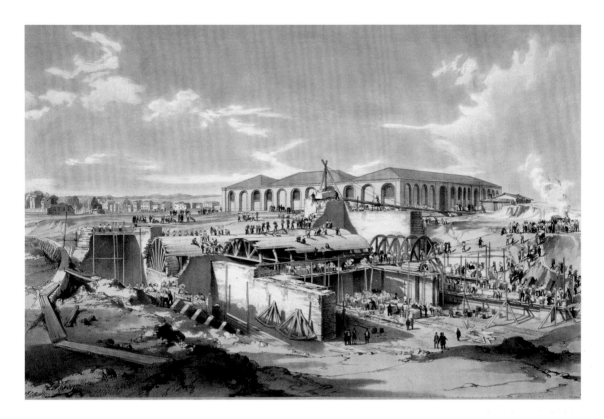

and further lacerated by the advent of the railways (see pages 154–177), which brought both industrial activity and poverty to the area. It is a setting to which Dickens returns in his fiction, setting the Cratchit home there in *A Christmas Carol* (1843) and describing railway development in *Dombey and Son* (1846-8) as it transformed the area, tearing through the close-packed streets,

> 'Houses were knocked down; streets broken through and stopped; deep pits and trenches dug in the ground; enormous heaps of earth and clay thrown up; buildings were undermined and shaking, propped by great beams of wood . . . Everywhere were bridges that led nowhere; thoroughfares that were wholly impassable . . . carcases of ragged tenements, and fragments of unfinished walls and arches, and piles of scaffolding, and wildernesses of bricks, and giant forms of cranes, and tripods straddling above nothing . . . In short, the yet unfinished and unopened Railroad was in progress . . .'

It was just such detailed descriptions of early

Building the Stationary Engine House, Camden Town, 28 April 1837, John Cooke Bourne

nineteenth-century London life which made his writing crackle. They also have proved an enduring legacy to later generations; Dickens lends sound, smell and colour to the monochrome photographs of the nineteenth-century streets.

Dickens began his writing career in 1833 at the age of twenty-one as a writer of sketches of London life, which later were collected and published as *Sketches by Boz*. In them he describes scenes, places, activities and characters with a wicked eye for humorous observation and a depth of detail. His words were further supported by the illustrations of George Cruikshank, who was already a well-established artist with a reputation for London scenes; Dickens's later works were enlivened by the work of his main illustrator, Hablôt Knight Browne, known as Phiz.

Sketches by Boz was followed by *The Pickwick Papers* (1836-7), *Oliver Twist* (1837-9) and *Nicholas Nickleby* (1838-9), all produced during the decade that saw the rise of Dickens's reputation as a highly popular writer of fiction. It was characteristic of him to have a number of projects in operation at the same time, beginning one work before he had completed the previous one. In 1836, for example, he was completing *The Pickwick Papers*, revising *Sketches* for another edition, writing a libretto for the London stage and all the while continuing his employment as a reporter for *The Morning Chronicle*.

This was also the time which saw his marriage, in 1836, to Catherine Hogarth, soon to be followed by the start of a family, and a move into their first family home at 48 Doughty Street in Bloomsbury in March 1837. Victoria became Queen in June of that year, and in July Euston Station opened as the terminus of the first inter-city railway line, from Birmingham to London. The combination of these three events brings together the new young Queen, the new mode of transport for the age to which she gives her name and the new young writer who was to chronicle that age and, especially, that of the development of its capital city. Walter Bagehot, the English economist and journalist, in a review of Dickens's work in 1858, wrote that Dickens's genius was

> '. . . *especially suited to the delineation of city life. London is like a newspaper; everything is there, and everything is disconnected. There is every kind of person in some houses; but there is no more connection between the houses than between the neighbours in the lists of "births, marriages, and deaths". As we change from the broad leader to the squalid police-report, we pass a corner and we are in a changed world. This is advantageous to Mr Dickens's genius. His memory is full of instances of old buildings and curious people, and he does not care to piece them together. On the contrary, each scene, to his mind, is a separate alertness of observation that is observable in those who live by it. He describes London like a special correspondent for posterity.'*

These three significant elements of nineteenth-century London were soon to be joined by a fourth: another means by which the age would be recorded for posterity. In a lecture to the Royal Society on 14 March 1839, Sir John Herschel first used the term 'photography' to describe the new process of fixing images, often called sun-pictures, on sensitive paper. The earliest photographic processes, the daguerrotype devised by the Frenchman Louis Daguerre, and the calotype, developed by Englishman William Henry Fox Talbot, were both introduced in this year.

From the outset London was the main focus of photographic activity in England. In October that same year, M. de St Croix was the first person to mount an exhibition of the French daguerrotype process in the capital, at the Royal Adelaide Gallery of Practical Science in the Strand. His photograph of Whitehall taken from Trafalgar Square (see page 27) shows the equestrian statue of Charles I and, in the hazy distance, the Banqueting House. There are figures of boys near the statue and cabs lined up at the roadside. Dickens describes the scene in *David Copperfield* as 'King Charles on horseback, surrounded by a maze of hackney-coaches, and looking anything but regal in a drizzling rain and a dark-brown fog'. Fox Talbot's early work also included photographs of the Banqueting House in Whitehall and a view of Westminster from Hungerford Market (where Charing Cross Station now stands), dating from June 1841. The new Houses of Parliament were being built at this time but had not risen sufficiently to be visible. The view from Hungerford Market shows the River Thames with wharves and jetties which existed until the construction of the embankments in the 1860s. In this area was Warren's blacking business where Dickens had been put to work in 1824, shortly after his twelfth birthday, when debt overtook the family.

By the 1840s, several photographic portrait studios had been established in central London; a daguerrotype studio run by Mr Richard Beard in the Polytechnic Institution, Cavendish Square, was in an attic 'with an extensive skylight to secure every available ray of the sun', the *Morning Herald* reported in March 1841. Beard's studio was popular with those who could afford the new portraiture; takings were often as much as £50 per day. By the mid-century more than sixty studios had opened, with Regent Street the focus of this new art of capturing images (see pages 178–195).

The new medium brought with it a new vocabulary, which was soon being used to describe other art forms, including that of powerful

Hungerford Stairs, 1820, George Harley

descriptive writing. Novelist George Eliot in 1856 praised Dickens's writing for using 'the delicate accuracy of a sun-picture'. Journalist H F Chorley wrote of Dickens giving one of his characters 'the immediate power of the daguerreotype' in the precision of her observation. George Brimley in *The Spectator* magazine in 1853 thought 'a daguerreotype of Fleet Street at noon-day would be the aptest symbol' for Dickens's powers of description. For William Forsyth in *Fraser's Magazine* in March 1857, Dickens 'daguerreotypes' individual characteristics and repeats them, just like reproducing an image from the same negative. R H Hutton, in *The Spectator* for June 18, 1870 acknowledged Dickens's 'power of observation so enormous that he could photograph almost everything he saw'.

Dickens's own response to photography was mixed. He generally found the process of having his likeness taken and exhibited to be unattractive, and advised others not to succumb to invitations to be photographed. He wrote to his friend, philanthropist Angela Burdett-Coutts, the wealthiest woman in England, on 23 May 1841,

'If anybody should entreat you to go to the Polytechnic Institution and have a Photographic likeness done – don't be prevailed upon, on any terms. The Sun is a great fellow in his way, but portrait painting is not his line. I speak from experience, having suffered dreadfully.'

However he was fascinated by the techniques and processes involved and included in his journal *Household Words* for 19 March 1853 an article by Henry Morley and W H Wills called 'Photography' which gives a description of a visit to a photographer's studio to see the process in action and a history of the

Portrait of Charles Dickens, 1861, John and Charles Watkins

development of the form. It concludes 'Photography is a young art, but from its present aspect we can judge what power it will have in its maturity'. Both *Household Words* and its successor *All the Year Round* include a number of pieces on the subject.

Dickens sent copies of his own photograph to applicants, and he also accepted Angela Burdett-Coutts's offer to have his son Walter taught photography before leaving for India in 1852. In December of that year he wrote to Miss Coutts praising the work of the photographer John E Mayall, for whom he had just recently sat,

'I am happy to say that the little piece of business between the Sun and myself, came off with the greatest success . . . The Artist who operated is quite a Genius in that way, and has acquired a large stock of a very singular knowledge of all the little eccentricities of the light and the instrument. The

consequence of which, is, that his results are very different from those of other men. I am disposed to think the portrait, by far the best specimen of anything in that way, I have ever seen.'

More significantly, Dickens describes his own method of work in photographic terms in a letter to W H Wills, his sub-editor on *Household Words*, of September 1858. The letter, written when he was undertaking his first provincial public reading tour, also refers positively to another photographer whose work he admired, John Watkins,

'I walked from Durham to Sunderland, and made a little fanciful photograph in my mind of Pit-Country, which will come well into H. W. one day. I couldn't help looking upon my mind as I was doing it, as a sort of capitally prepared and highly sensitive plate. And I said, without the least conceit (as Watkins might have said of a plate of his) "it really is a pleasure to work with you, you receive the impression so nicely".'

It is this combination, of capturing the realism of the moment as in a photograph and bringing to it qualities of imagination in depiction, which identify the essential qualities of Dickens's art. One of his other journalistic contributors, John Hollingshead, writing in his own memoir *My Lifetime* in 1895 looked back on Dickens in this way,

'His walks were always walks of observation, through parts of London that he wanted to study. His brain must have been like a photographic lens, and fully studded with "snap-shots". The streets and the people, the houses and the roads, the cabs, the buses and the traffic, the characters in the shops and on the footways, the whole kaleidoscope of Metropolitan existence . . .'

This capacity for imaginative observation provides the keynote for his depiction of London, as for all else in his output. In 'Meditations in Monmouth Street', from 1836, Dickens describes an area well-known as a street of second-hand clothes shops (see page 71), near Seven Dials, a very poor, criminalised area at the time. (Monmouth Street later became part of Shaftesbury Avenue.) The shops in Monmouth Street would at that

LONDON going out of Town — or — The March of Bricks & Mortar!

time have had old clothes hanging up outside them. Dickens begins by observing some of the garments on offer and then allows his imagination to develop the life stories of previous owners of the clothing,

> 'The first was a patched and much-soiled skeleton suit . . . It had belonged to a town boy, we could see; there was a shortness about the legs and arms of the suit; and a bagging at the knees, peculiar to the rising youth of London streets. A small day-school he had been at, evidently. If it had been a regular boys' school they wouldn't have let him play on the floor so much, and rub his knees so white. He had an indulgent mother too, and plenty of halfpence, as the numerous smears of some sticky substance about the pockets, and just below the chin, which even the salesman's skill could not succeed in disguising, sufficiently betokened . . .'

Dickens always acknowledged how important London was to his creative processes, mentioning his need for the imagery that the city laid out for him on his numerous walks. On 30 August 1846, he wrote to his friend and later biographer, John Forster, about the

London Going Out of Town or the March of Bricks and Mortar, 1829, George Cruikshank

difficulties he was experiencing with his writing of *Dombey and Son*, in 'the absence of streets . . . A day in London sets me up again and starts me. But the toil and labour of writing, day after day, without that magic lantern, is IMMENSE!!' Again, it is notable that he uses a visual reference – the magic lantern, used to project images for entertainment – to define his relation with his great inspiration. His friend, the actor William Charles Macready, described Dickens as having 'a clutching eye' – referring to the writer's uncanny ability to see and record his vision in a photographic-like way.

The London which Dickens described, and which the photographs in this book capture, expanded quickly during the nineteenth century. It was a city of just under a million at the beginning of the century, increasing to 1.5 million by the 1820s when Dickens moved there as boy. By the mid-century, the year of the Great Exhibition of 1851, London's population had increased to 2.5 million and by the early 1870s was heading for 3.5 million.

Three boys and a policeman, c.1850, Hablôt Knight Browne ('Phiz')

Despite all of the horrors of the high rates of infant mortality and the epidemic outbreaks of deadly cholera in the nineteenth century, the general demographic trend during the period was for an increase in births greater than that of deaths. But a very large part of the population increase was due to migration, not only from other parts of the British mainland, but also from Ireland, especially during the Hungry Forties when harvest failures brought famine to the island, and from Europe. The Dickens family themselves were one such group of migrants, and it is interesting to note how often Dickens returns in his novels to the idea of his characters entering London for the first time, as we have seen in *David Copperfield*. It is also true for Pip in *Great Expectations*, whose hopes of London are disappointed by the reality. On arrival there from Kent, he finds the city 'rather ugly, crooked, narrow and dirty', and himself 'scared by the immensity of London'.

The scale of the city's growth led Dickens to ponder the social problems of mass migration – the loss of identity, of community in the ever-expanding and increasingly impersonal metropolis. In an essay called 'Thoughts About People', published in April 1835, he writes,

'It is strange with how little notice, good, bad, or indifferent, a man may live and die in London. He awakens no sympathy in the breast of any single person; his existence is a matter of interest to no one save himself; he cannot be said to be forgotten when he dies, for no one remembered him when he was alive. There is a numerous class of people in this great metropolis who seem not to possess a single friend, and whom nobody appears to care for. Urged by imperative necessity in the first instance, they have resorted to London in search of employment, and the means of subsistence . . . (and) have become lost . . . in the crowd and turmoil . . .'

Innocent people come to the city because it seems to offer them a means of survival; the city then destroys them. 'London,' Dickens wrote to politician and fellow author Edward Bulwer-Lytton in February 1851, 'is a vile place'. Dickens often described the city as hungry, a ravening beast which was capable of devouring all who entered. In *Dombey and Son* he has a character observe,

'the stragglers who came wandering into London, by the great highway hard by, and who, footsore and weary, and gazing fearfully at the huge town before them, as if foreboding that their misery there would be but as a drop of water in the sea, or as a grain of sea-sand on the shore, went shrinking on . . . Day after day, such travellers crept past, but always…in one direction – always towards the town. Food for the hospitals, the churchyards, the prisons, the river, fever, madness, vice, and death – they passed on to the monster, roaring in the distance, and were lost.'

Again, it was this ability to depict the reality of London life which allowed Dickens's huge audiences to identify themselves, their families or their friends or neighbours in his writings, particularly in his detailed descriptions of the lives of the poor. There were few photographic images of London poor (see page 58) during the early days of the new medium: those original 'sun portraits' were the prerogative of the wealthy. Dickens's word pictures were the place of record for humbler lives, and struck a chord with all who could afford to follow his stories serialised in the weekly journals; the same 'lower classes' who would, years later, file past his open grave in Westminster Abbey, leaving hand-tied offerings of humble wild flowers.

After population growth, the next significant change in the fabric of London between 1822 and 1870 was that caused by the coming of the railways. All of London's main railway termini were built between 1836 and 1874, with the exception of Blackfriars (1886) and Marylebone (1899). With them came an increase in crossing-points on the Thames. London's urban sprawl began to reach ever outwards, enveloping green fields and dairy pastures, covering over meandering streams and brooks and realigning the natural lie of the land. More rapid communication and transport came hand in hand with a quickening of the pace of life, spurred on by the regulation of time itself as clocks were universally regimented to record accurate departures and arrivals on the railways.

In his great mid-century novel *Bleak House*, Dickens satirises those members of society and of government who are determined not 'to receive any impress from the moving age', in other words, not to respond to social and other forces of change. That could never be said of him. In *Dombey and Son*, written in the middle of the railway boom, he responds powerfully to the changes going on in London's landscape as whole communities are displaced for the railway (see pages 154–177). But for long after the arrival of railways in London, the transport of an earlier time was still in evidence in the large number of coaching inns across the city (see page 74). When David Copperfield arrives in London from Suffolk, he arrives at one such inn 'in the Whitechapel district… called the Blue Bull, or the Blue Boar'. Photographs have recorded these evocations of a past age for us; Dickens records them through memorable characters such as stagecoach driver Tony Weller, father of Sam, the 'boots' at the White Hart in Borough High Street in *The Pickwick Papers* (the fifteenth-century inn now remembered only in the name White Hart Yard). Weller senior had strong views about the new means of transport,

'. . . And as to the ingein, – a nasty, wheezin', creakin', gaspin', puffin', bustin' monster, alvays

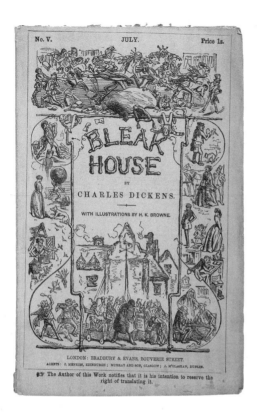

Cover of *Bleak House* part work, 1852

The economic boom brought improvements to many inner urban areas, with much of central London being rebuilt as the disruption of the rail incursions prompted long-needed reconstruction of the city's decrepit and outdated infrastructure. The London captured in early Victorian photographs (see pages 57–73) records an environment of narrow alleyways, courts and slum dwellings which were soon to disappear, a city of twists and turns providing an ideal bolt-hole for the criminal, which were bewildering to the visitor, as Dickens describes in *Martin Chuzzlewit*,

> '*You couldn't walk about Todgers's neighbourhood, as you could in any other neighbourhood. You groped your way for an hour through lanes and byways, and court-yards, and passages; and you never once emerged upon anything that might be reasonably called a street. A kind of resigned distraction came over the stranger as he trod those devious mazes, and, giving himself up for lost, went in and out and round about and quietly turned back again when he came to a dead wall or was stopped by an iron railing . . . Instances were known of people who, being asked to dine at Todgers's, had travelled round and round for a weary time, with its very chimney-pots in view; and finding it, at last, impossible of attainment, had gone home again with a gentle melancholy on their spirits, tranquil and uncomplaining. . . . Todgers's was in a labyrinth, whereof the mystery was known but to a chosen few.*'

out o' breath, vith a shiny green-and-gold back, like a unpleasant beetle in that 'ere gas magnifier, – as to the ingein as is alvays a pourin' out red-hot coals at night, and black smoke in the day, the sensiblest thing it does, in my opinion, is, ven there's somethin' in the vay, and it sets up that 'ere frightful scream vich seems to say, "Now here's two hundred and forty passengers in the very greatest extremity o' danger, and here's their two hundred and forty screams in vun!" '

Of course, there was another side to the massive changes which London was undergoing: improved means of communication stimulated the economy. London was a great commercial city. Everywhere one looked there was advertising (see page 105). Indeed, Dickens's own novels were commercial commodities, published as monthly parts, each one containing two or three chapters, a couple of illustrations, and some wonderful advertising. He even employed his own image in advertising.

New roads were driven through, like New Oxford Street in 1847, linking Oxford Street and High Holborn, and removing one of the worst rookeries of vice and poverty around St Giles's High Street. However, as Dickens pointed out, many such reconstruction projects resulted simply in moving the inhabitants on to other, ultimately worse, pockets of degradation, as he noted in *Household Words* of June 14, 1851, in an article called 'On Duty with Inspector Field',

> '*Thus we make our New Oxford Streets and our other new streets, never heeding, never asking, where the wretches whom we clear out, crowd.*
>   *Saint Giles's church clock, striking eleven, hums*

Charles Dickens, 1839, after William Finden's engraving

The Pickwickians handkerchief, c.1840

through our hand from the dilapidated door of a dark outhouse as we open it, and are stricken back by the pestilent breath that issues from within . . . let us look!

Ten, twenty, thirty – who can count them! Men, women, children, for the most part naked, heaped upon the floor like maggots in a cheese! Ho! In that dark corner yonder! Does anybody lie there? Me sir, Irish me, a widder, with six children. And yonder? Me sir, Irish me, with me wife and eight poor babes . . .'

From the lowest slum to the seat of power, London was rebuilt through the nineteenth century. At Whitehall, Parliament Square was redeveloped and the slow reconstruction of the Parliament buildings was underway. The new Palace of Westminster was designed by Charles Barry and Augustus Welby Pugin in Gothic Revival style to marry the new structure with the surviving medieval buildings from the 1834 fire that burnt down the old palace where Dickens had worked as a Parliamentary reporter. Other old haunts of his were also redeveloped, some to his evident pleasure.

Dickens was a keen supporter of the plan to create embankments along the Thames (see pages 278–282), thus reclaiming land and creating protection for property close to the previously open and shelving riverside, particularly at Hungerford Stairs, where he had worked in the rat-infested blacking factory and where the new Charing Cross Station was constructed. He told his friend, and biographer, John Forster,

'Until Old Hungerford Market was pulled down, until Old Hungerford Stairs were destroyed, and the very nature of the ground changed, I never had the courage to go back to the place where my servitude began. I never saw it. I could not endure to go near it.'

Dickens may not have frequented the area, but many of his characters did. Mr Micawber set off with his family for their new life in Australia from Hungerford Stairs which led up from the river to the Strand, and Dickens describes how the last days of the emigrants were spent 'in a little, dirty, tumbledown public-house, which in those days was close to the stairs, and whose protruding wooden rooms hung over the river'.

The Pool, 1859, James McNeill Whistler

The Thames itself occupies a dominant position in Dickens's imagination (see pages 112–137). It was a thoroughfare, a trade route, a dark and brooding presence and, for much of the century, also a source of disease, in reality little more than an open sewer, until the building of the embankments under the aegis of Joseph Bazalgette, chief engineer of the Metropolitan Board of Works. The embankments encased a new sewerage system, which removed the effluent from the river and took it downstream, away from the offended nostrils of MPs whose outrage at the Great Stink of the summer of 1858, when the stench from untreated human waste swilling about in the polluted river was so strong that Parliamentary business had to be suspended, had hastened sanitary reform. Though he did not live to see the construction of the embankments completed, Dickens wrote in a letter in January 1869 that he regarded it as 'the finest public work yet done'.

Dickens's last completed work, *Our Mutual Friend*, focuses on the lives of those who make a living from what can be found in the river, including human remains, and in the novel Dickens graphically describes the riverside area,

> 'The wheels rolled on . . . down by the Monument and by the Tower, and by the Docks; down by Ratcliffe, and by Rotherhithe; down by where accumulated scum of humanity seemed to be washed from higher grounds, like so much moral sewage, and to be pausing until its own weight forced it over the bank and sunk it in the river. In and out among the vessels that seemed to have got ashore, and houses that seemed to have got afloat – among bow-splits staring into windows, and windows staring into ships – the wheels rolled on, until they stopped at a dark corner, river-washed and otherwise not washed at all, where the boy alighted and opened the door.'

Elsewhere in the same tale it is a 'dirty indecorous drab of a river' or it has 'an awful look... as if the spectres of suicides were holding (the reflected lights) to show where they went down'. Dickens also uses the riverside powerfully in *Oliver Twist*, where

he sets the concluding movement of the novel in Jacob's Island, Bermondsey, the scene of Fagin's arrest and Bill Sikes's death,

A Bird's Eye View of Smithfield Market taken from the Bear and Ragged Staff, 1811, Thomas Rowlandson and Auguste Charles Pugin

> '*In such a neighbourhood, beyond Dockhead in the Borough of Southwark, stands Jacob's Island, surrounded by a muddy ditch, six or eight feet deep and fifteen or twenty wide when the tide is in, once called Mill Pond, but known in the days of this story as Folly Ditch. It is a creek or inlet from the Thames, and can always be filled at high water by opening the sluices at the Lead Mills from which it took its old name. At such times, a stranger, looking from one of the wooden bridges thrown across it at Mill Lane, will see the inhabitants of the houses on either side lowering from their back doors and windows, buckets, pails, domestic utensils of all kinds, in which to haul the water up; and when his eye is turned from these operations to the houses themselves, his utmost astonishment will be excited by the scene before him. Crazy*

> *wooden galleries common to the backs of half-a-dozen houses, with holes from which to look upon the slime beneath; windows, broken and patched, with poles thrust out, on which to dry the linen that is never there; rooms so small, so filthy, so confined, that the air would seem too tainted even for the dirt and squalor which they shelter; wooden chambers thrusting themselves out above the mud, and threatening to fall into it – as some have done; dirt-besmeared walls and decaying foundations; every repulsive lineament of poverty, every loathsome indication of filth, rot, and garbage; all these ornament the banks of Folly Ditch.*'

Dickens was anxious to see reform in the conditions of life in London; he was particularly keen to lend his considerable influence to the question of Smithfield Market, which in the early part of the nineteenth century was an open-air beast market. There were growing protests about the condition of the market, the animals and the surrounding streets, from the 1820s. Dickens describes it vividly in *Oliver Twist*,

> *'The ground was covered, nearly ankle-deep, with filth and mire; a thick steam, perpetually rising from the reeking bodies of the cattle, and mingling with the fog . . . hung heavily above. Countrymen, butchers, drovers, hawkers, boys, thieves, idlers, and vagabonds of every low grade, were mingled together in a mass; the whistling of drovers, the barking dogs, the bellowing and plunging of the oxen, the bleating of sheep, the grunting and squeaking of pigs, the cries of hawkers, the shouts, oaths, and quarrelling on all sides; the ringing of bells and roar of voices, that issued from every public-house; the crowding, pushing, driving, beating, whooping and yelling; the hideous and discordant dim that resounded from every corner of the market; and the unwashed, unshaven, squalid, and dirty figures constantly running to and fro, and bursting in and out of the throng; rendered it a stunning and bewildering scene, which quite confounded the senses.'*

He returns to the market when Pip arrives in London in *Great Expectations*, 'So, I came into Smithfield; and the shameful place, being all asmear with fat and blood and foam, seemed to stick to me'. Animals were driven by drovers through the narrow streets surrounding Smithfield until they reached the market. In 1839 total sales for the year included some 180,000 cattle, over 250,000 pigs and almost 1,400,000 sheep. Conditions and cruelty were appalling. There were more animals than could be accommodated, so they were kept in off-droves, penned into nearby streets. By 1850 there was a proposal that the market should be closed and moved out of the City. The City Corporation's main policy-making body, the Court of Common Council, opposed this suggestion. Dickens wrote an article for *Household Words* in March 1851, called 'A Monument of French Folly', in which he drew unfavourable contrasts between the sanitary and efficient way the meat markets of Paris operated and the chaotic horror of Smithfield, with its entrenched self-interest on the part of the Corporation.

The reformers prevailed and in 1852 the Smithfield Market Removal Act was passed, providing for the beast market to be held in Copenhagen Fields in Islington. Named the Caledonian Meat Market, this opened in 1855. The present market building in Smithfield, London Central Markets, was built between 1866 and 1868 to Sir Horace Jones's design (see pages 96–97), so Dickens would have seen its construction.

Another significant change in London during Dickens's time was the establishment of the Metropolitan Police Force in 1829, seven years after his arrival in the capital. Later, in 1842, the Detective Police was established and Dickens's interest in the way the force operated, and especially his friendship with, and admiration of, Inspector Charles Frederick Field, led to his making nocturnal explorations of the city's dens of vice and crime, in company with Field and his officers. These visits appear as a series of articles called 'On Duty with Inspector Field', but Field is also thought to be the inspiration for Inspector Bucket in *Bleak House*.

It is well documented that many of Dickens's characters – like the writer himself – are fascinated, even haunted, by images of prison and execution. It is one aspect of the 'attraction of repulsion' which Dickens's biographer Forster identifies as a key element in his art. The Old Bailey, Dickens writes, was 'a kind of deadly inn-yard from which pale travellers set out continually, in carts and coaches, on a violent passage into the other world'. Dickens knew well, too, the Compter debtor's prison on the corner of Giltspur Street in Smithfield, and the Fleet prison, on the eastern bank of the Fleet River on what is now Farringdon Street, where Mr Pickwick is sent when he refuses to pay the damages after the trial for breach of promise. The Middlesex House of Correction, on the site of the present Mount Pleasant Post Office complex, is just a few minutes' walk away from Dickens's home in Doughty Street, and he visited it several times to observe the operation of the reforms introduced by its governor George Laval Chesterton.

Dickens's closest links, however, were with the Marshalsea, the debtors' prison which moved into a new building on Borough High Street, Southwark in 1811, and which was where his father was sent for some months when young Charles was twelve years old.

Dickens visited his family in Marshalsea on Sundays, when not working at the blacking factory, and he later faithfully recorded the prison scenes in *Little Dorrit*,

> *'Thirty years ago there stood, a few doors short of the church of Saint George, in the borough of Southwark, on the left-hand side of the way going southward, the Marshalsea Prison. It had stood there many years before, and it remained there some years afterwards; but it is gone now, and the world is none the worse without it.'*

In the preface he wrote for the novel in 1857 he further emphasised the location,

> *'But, whosoever goes into Marshalsea Place, turning out of Angel Court, leading to Bermondsey, will find his feet on the very paving-stones of the extinct Marshalsea jail; will see its narrow yard to the right and to the left, very little altered if at all, except that the walls were lowered when the place got free; will look upon rooms in which the debtors lived; and will stand among the crowding ghosts of many miserable years.'*

It is, however, Newgate (see pages 175 and 176) which exerts exceptional power over Dickens's imagination. Executions took place in public until 1868 (Dickens was vocal in campaigning for their taking place inside prison) were carried out in Newgate Street, where animals bought at Smithfield would come for slaughter, usually at eight in the morning, a fact observed by Nancy to Bill Sikes as they hear the bells of the church of St Sepulchre, at the top of the Old Bailey. It was past this church that condemned felons would be taken by cart to Tyburn before executions moved here. In *Barnaby Rudge*, Dickens describes the burning of the old Newgate Gaol during the Gordon Riots of 1780, creating a glow so great that 'the church clock of St Sepulchre's, so often pointing to the hour of death, was legible as in broad day'. The rebuilt prison lasted from 1783 to demolition in 1902.

The other great City of London landmark which Dickens uses is that of St Paul's Cathedral (see pages 28 and 29). In *Great Expectations* Pip observes 'the

Criminal broadsheet recounting the trial and execution of Courvoisier, 1840

EXECUTION

OF COURVOISIER,

Who was Executed on Monday July the 6th, 1840, for the Wilful Murder of Lord William Russell, on Wednesday, May 6th, at his Residence, 14, Norfolk-Street, Park-lane, London.

Since the period of his condemnation the convict Courvoisier, maintained the same apparent indisposition to the dreadful death he was about to undergo as he had previous to his trial, and appeared to have had an amusement in inventing various and false versions of his confessions; the one day declaring that Lord Russell caught him in the act of plundering, the next that his Lordship never left his bed, and the third that he had buried some money in the cell, at Bow-street, so that at length nothing could be relied upon in any of his statements, except the fact of his having committed the murder; his confessions being so various, and proved to contain so many falsehoods. This hardihood continued until the visit of his Uncle, with whom he had two interviews, in the presence of the Chaplain of Newgate.

His Uncle is a person of great respectability, and has been for eighteen years in the service of Sir George Beaumont; these interviews there is every reason to believe, were productive of the most beneficial results, as the convict appeared awakened to his awful situation and explained many of the inconsistences in his confession.

On Sunday the Rev Mr. Carver, the Ordinary of Newgate, preached the condemned Sermon, in the Chapel of Newgate, to the prisoner, and a very crowded auditory; taking his text from Job, chap. xxiv., ver 21, 22

The Rev. Gentleman entered in the most full manner into the enormity of the prisoner's crime, who from motives of avarice and plunder had shed the blood, not only of an aged and unoffended nobleman but that nobleman his kind and indulgent master, who intrusted his life in his hands, yet, whom he murdered while in the calm repose of sleep. After warning the other prisoners from the commission of so heinous a crime and detailing by the prisoner's example the certainty of guilt, however cunningly devised and speedily punished by Law, he endeavoured to awaken in the Culprit that although here death was certain, yet, however enormous his guilt, by throwing himself by due repentance upon the mercies of the Redeemer, he might still inherit everlasting life in the world to come. The prisoner appeared to feel deeply throughout, and there was scarcely a dry eye among the crowded congregation. During the last night for the unhappy malefactor he slept for about three hours, and on awaking, anxiously enquired what time it was.

THE OLD BAILEY

From an early hour this morning the workmen where busily engaged in making the necessary preparations for the awful ceremony which was about to take place; barriers were placed at the end of Newgate Street, and in all the other thoroughfares to prevent accidents from the denseness of the crowd, and at about 6 o'clock, the engine of death was wheeled out of the great gates and placed in front of the Debtors door; large bodies of police also now marched to various stations in order to preserve order. The crowd now began to assemble and the whole of the area was speedily filled by the dense multitude; every avenue, window, and house-stop, which could command a view of the place of execution, being crowded with spectators.

THE GAOL

At ten minutes past 7 o'clock, the Sheriffs and other authorities arrived at the Gaol and having proceeded to the press room, the culprit was summoned from his cell and conveyed to the Chapel, where he received the Sacrament, having declared his deep penitence for his crime; he was then conducted to the press-room, where the awful preparations for death, by pinioning his arms, placing the fatal cap on his head, &c, commenced. The prisoner appeared overcome by his situation and wept bitterly.

The Prison Bell now began to toll, and the preparations being complete, the last procession moved towards the drop, the Chaplain reading the Funeral Service. Upon the prisoner's arriving on the drop an audible shudder ran throughout the crowd. He took his stand on the drop, the fatal noose was shortly adjusted, the bolt drawn, and the unhappy man was launched into eternity, and in a few minutes ceased to exist.

John Bonner, Printer, 31, Back Street, Bristol.

great black dome of St Paul's bulging at me from behind a grim stone building which a bystander said was Newgate prison'. Jo, the crossing-sweeper in *Bleak House* who 'don't know nothink', and dies succumbing to pneumonia, the disease so rife in nineteenth-century London, observes St Paul's from his position on Blackfriars Bridge. Dickens describes Jo

> '*munching and gnawing, looking up at the great cross on the summit of St Paul's Cathedral, glittering above a red and violet tinted cloud of smoke. From the boy's face one might suppose that sacred emblem to be, in his eyes, the crowning confusion of the great confused city, so golden, so high up, so far out of his reach.*'

The symbolism to which Dickens puts St Paul's is clear: unattainable peace and comfort, a place surrounded by suffering and cruelty.

The link between Dickens and London continued to his death on 9 June 1870. His own wishes were that he might be buried quietly in 'the small graveyard under Rochester Castle wall'. Rochester, in the Kentish countryside, where he had spent happy years in his boyhood, and to which he had returned, a highly successful man, and which he described as being 'the birthplace of (his) fancy', or his imagination: that imagination which grew and matured in London. The outpouring of national and international grief at his death was enormous, and spanned the entire social spectrum. *The Times* newspaper took the lead in campaigning for national public recognition of his life and achievements. There clearly had to be some degree of reconciliation between his wishes and the very understandable need to offer the opportunity for public homage and grieving.

On Tuesday 14 June, with the knowledge only of those who were to take part, a small group of family and friends arrived at the Dean's Yard entrance to Westminster Abbey in three mourning coaches, and Dickens's burial took place in the otherwise empty abbey church. The grave was left open for the rest of the day. Mourners came to visit later that day, then all of the following day, the Wednesday, and the grave was still kept open on Thursday, the numbers were so great. When it was closed the mourners still came. The stone bears simply his name and the dates of his

birth and death. On 20 June 1870, *The Times* printed the text of the sermon delivered by Benjamin Jowett, of Balliol College, at the funeral service. The sermon captures the astonishing depth of feeling which Dickens evoked in those who knew him – and all who believed they knew him, from those wonderful creations of his mind and heart presented in his writings. It is this legacy which spans the years and is still accessible to all of us, in a world very different to that in which he lived.

All of his novels include, to a greater or lesser degree, references to London, as does most of his journalism. There are guidebooks to 'Dickens's London', significant sections in books on 'Literary London', and professionally-guided walks available to explore places connected with the novels. Histories of the city all make significant reference to Dickens when presenting their accounts of nineteenth-century London. Blue plaques on London buildings commemorate places of importance in his life and writings. All of this shows us that the connection between the creations of the writer's imagination and the real world of the metropolis is enormously strong.

Dickens's London is a world to which we can return through the images in this volume. One is a photograph by John Thomson (see page 100) showing porters at work in Covent Garden market in 1877, only seven years after Dickens's death. Covent Garden holds a position of great significance for Dickens: to visit there 'perfectly entranced him with pleasure', Forster tells us. In 1823, soon after his arrival in London as a young boy, Dickens would visit his uncle Thomas Barrow in his lodgings in Gerrard Street, Soho, above a bookshop run by Mrs Manson. She would lend the boy books and one which fascinated him was *Broad Grins* by George Colman which contained descriptions of Covent Garden. Dickens ran down to the market to compare it with the description and there inhaled 'the flavour of the faded cabbage-leaves as if it were the very breath of comic fiction'. Covent Garden appears in almost all of his novels; Wellington Street in Covent Garden was the site of the offices of his two journals and it is from there that he describes the Uncommercial Traveller setting out on his excursions. Covent Garden Theatre, originally built in 1731, was burnt down in 1806, rebuilt and burnt down again in 1856, to be rebuilt two years later. Dickens visited the ruins of the recently-destroyed theatre four days after the fire, when he returned from Paris. It was at Covent Garden Theatre that Dickens arranged to be auditioned for a stage career in 1832 but was prevented by a heavy cold from attending. The area had connections, too, that would have remained with Dickens long into his later life because, whilst working at Warren's blacking factory in 1824, the business transferred to premises in Chandos Street, Covent Garden, and passers-by would stop to observe, through the ground-floor windows, the skilful workmanship of the boys labelling, wrapping and tying up the pots of shoe-blacking.

Two of the Covent Garden porters in John Thomson's photograph are looking directly towards the camera, directly at us, the observers. The Victorians are the first of our ancestors with whom we can make that degree of contact through images that capture a moment in time, much as Charles Dickens captures their world in words. The canvas of the metropolis reinforces the most powerful personal and social concerns of this great writer, who both celebrates the city and helps create our vision of the modern metropolis. For Dickens did reflect the actuality of the city. He saw, and wrote about it, as a place of astonishing, overwhelming contrasts, extreme wealth alongside degrading, bitter poverty. He shows us the enticing city which becomes a trap and labyrinth: a very modern concept, brought sharply into focus through the fog-bound world of *Bleak House*. In his last complete novel, *Our Mutual Friend*, Dickens paints a word-picture of a modern, almost surreal, cityscape of mounds of rubbish with a dark, destructive river snaking its way through it.

Photographers began to capture images of the city from 1839. By the time that Dickens died in 1870, it was perhaps less imperative for writers to capture the city in prose as Dickens had; his 'photographic' recollections of city life were there in black and white for all to view. The city remained much as he would recognise it to the end of the Victorian age in 1901, the era which is illustrated by the photographs included in this volume. They show Victorian London, indissolubly linked with its greatest writer.

Charles Dickens's grave in Poet's Corner,
Westminster Abbey, c.1870

LANDMARKS (OLD LONDON)

When Dickens arrived in London in 1822 as a boy, the skyline was dominated by Westminster Abbey in the west and St Paul's Cathedral in the central part of the City. In the first half of the eighteenth century, the abbey's two west towers had been constructed to the designs of Nicholas Hawksmoor. The most sumptuous and theatrically extravagant coronation of the nineteenth century was that of George IV, Queen Victoria's uncle. The king was personally involved in planning the detail of the ceremony which took place in the abbey on 19 July 1821. He wanted a spectacle which would uphold and emphasise England's status as the most powerful country in Europe following the defeat of Napoleon at Waterloo in 1815. Queen Victoria's coronation was a less grand affair though it was arranged so that she could be seen by her subjects as she processed to and from the Abbey. At 10 a.m. on 28 June 1838, the Queen left Buckingham Palace for the Abbey, travelling in the state coach up Constitution Hill, along Piccadilly, down St James's Street and across Trafalgar Square to the Abbey.

Walter Thornbury writing in 1878 described St Paul's Cathedral as 'the very palladium of modern London'. Visitors to the city were impressed by its scale and architectural design though they criticised the narrow lanes and contracted space surrounding it. The two most prominent state funerals of the century were held at the cathedral. When George III heard of Nelson's death at the battle of Trafalgar he ordered that 'the body of the British hero should be buried in St Paul's at the public expense, with military and national honours'. In 1806, the procession accompanying Nelson's funeral cortège included ten thousand soldiers. The Duke of Wellington's funeral in 1852 was possibly even more impressive. An immense crowd, estimated at one and a half million,

lined the streets to pay their respects to the military hero as his coffin was carried from Horse Guards to the cathedral. A magazine article, however, entitled 'Trading in Death' in Dickens's *Household Words* was critical of the commercialisation and political nature of the event as well as the 'barbarous show and expense' attached to funerals in general.

The Tower of London was a landmark that fascinated Victorians. Guidebooks reflected the historical themes that were particularly appealing, 'the scenes of oppression and misery which its walls have witnessed, crowd on the recollection; the sight of its exterior defences which seem to indicate strength and security, leads the imagination to penetrate those chambers which were, for centuries, the prisons not only of bad and designing men, but of the great and the good, the victims alternately of tyranny and anarchy.'

In 1841, the Tower was struck by a serious fire. It started in the Bowyer Tower and quickly spread through the Grand Storehouse threatening the Martin Tower, which housed the Jewel House, and the White Tower. In the scorching heat the lead pipes of the White Tower melted and stocks of ammunition had to be removed from the basement. The Grand Storehouse was utterly destroyed, together with its collection of historic arms and armour. The fire at the Tower precipitated a programme of repairs and rebuilding which continued throughout the century. The Waterloo Barracks, housing 1,000 soldiers was built on the site of the Grand Storehouse and the moat, a health hazard and source of cholera, was drained. The Tower of London was restored under the direction of the architect Anthony Salvin, an authority on castle architecture. His aim was to re-create the Tower's original appearance as a formidable fortress.

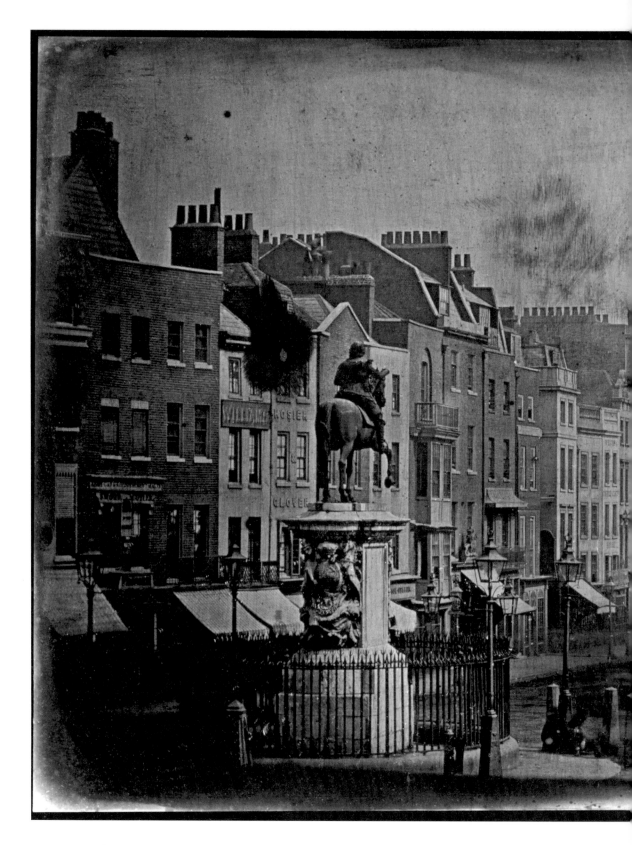

WHITEHALL, 1839

This daguerreotype taken by M. de St Croix has been reversed to show the view the right way round. It is one of the earliest photographs of the capital. Taken from Trafalgar Square, the view looks west down Whitehall with the Banqueting House in the distance on the left. Le Seur's equestrian statue of Charles I in the foreground was observed by David Copperfield in Dickens's novel: he 'stood peeping out of window at King Charles on horseback, surrounded by a maze of hackney-coaches, and looking anything but regal in a drizzling rain and a dark-brown fog'. Mr Jingle, in his distinctive staccato phrases, in *The Pickwick Papers* says to Mr Pickwick 'Looking at Whitehall, sir? – fine place – little window – somebody else's head off there, eh, sir? – he didn't keep a sharp look-out enough either – eh, Sir, eh?'

Previous page: **TEMPLE BAR, C. 1875**

In this view of Temple Bar, looking west, it is just possible to make out part of the church of St Clement Danes through the central gate. In 1860 Dickens proposed to meet Wilkie Collins at the Cock Tavern for a 'British Steak'. The tavern was rebuilt on the south side in the 1880s and still survives today. The buildings beyond Temple Bar on the right had been demolished and work recently started on the new Courts of Justice.

VIEW OF ST PAUL'S, C.1865

The photograph above reveals the buildings fronting the north side of Cannon Street close to St Paul's Cathedral. The tall structure in the foreground is the premises of Spreckley, White and Lewis (formerly Beloe and Spreckley) one of London's largest wholesale textile warehouses, specialising especially in mantles, jackets and millinery.

ST PAUL'S CATHEDRAL, 1854

This early photograph wonderfully captures the pre-eminence of the cathedral on the City of London's skyline. Charles Dickens would have known this view well with the riverside warehouses and wharves and the blanket of roofs behind partly shrouded in smoke. The immensity of the dome of St. Paul's seems almost to float above the cityscape. In the centre foreground, Blundell, Spence & Co.'s Anchor Wharf has been painted white. This was a Hull-based paint and oil manufacturer known especially for its patent palm oil used for lubricating machinery such as steam engines. To the right stands the bottle warehouse of Ayre and Calder. In *David Copperfield*, the hero is put to work in Murdstone and Grinby's bottle warehouse in the vicinity of Blackfriars.

St Paul's Cathedral, c.1860-1875

These photographs show the low and generally uniform height of the buildings surrounding the cathedral with just the towers and steeples of the City of London's other churches punctuating the skyline. The crossing-sweeper Jo, in Dickens's *Bleak House*, considers the skyline of London from Blackfriars Bridge, 'And there he sits, munching and gnawing, and looking up at the great Cross on the summit of St Paul's Cathedral, glittering above a red and violet-tinted cloud of smoke. From the boy's face one might suppose that sacred emblem to be, in his eyes, the crowning confusion of the great, confused city; so golden, so high up, so far out of his reach'.

WATERGATE OF YORK HOUSE, C.1880

In 1860, in Dickens's weekly magazine *All the Year Round*, an article described an old hidden part of London known as the Precinct, close to the river and near where the magazine was published. This and the surrounding area south of the Strand, near Waterloo Bridge, fascinated Dickens. It had once been occupied by grand palaces with gardens that ran down to the river. By the early Victorian period, it had become slightly ramshackle and decayed. A few relics of its earlier grandeur survived such as the 'beautiful water-gate at the end of Buckingham Street', all that was left of the Palace of the Duke of Buckingham. The building of the Victoria Embankment reclaimed the foreshore in front of the gate so that it now stands at quite some distance from the river.

THE MONUMENT, C.1875

In *Martin Chuzzlewit*, the Monument, the column commemorating the Great Fire of London, was located near to Todgers Commercial Boarding House which was run by Mrs Todgers and where Pecksniff and his daughters stayed. Tom Pinch, finding himself alongside the entrance to the Monument when lost in the city, overheard the doorman tell a couple that it cost a 'tanner' each (six old pence) to climb up to the top. With some 311 steps, the doorman laughed to himself stating that, 'It's worth twice the money to stop here'.

TEMPLE BAR, C.1860-1878

Temple Bar marks the western edge of the City of London where Fleet Street becomes the Strand and was the last of the gateways into the City to survive. Designed by Sir Christopher Wren and constructed between 1669 and 1672, by the middle of the nineteenth century it had become a hindrance to traffic. Dickens described Temple Bar at the start of *Bleak House*, as a 'leaden-headed old obstruction, appropriate ornament for the threshold of a leaden-headed old corporation.' In *A Tale of Two Cities* he reminded readers of the tradition of placing the heads of executed traitors on the top of it. Tellson's Bank, based on Child's Bank and featured in the same novel, was 'an old-fashioned place' situated just by Temple Bar and used the upper parts of the Bar as a store for financial documents. Demolished in 1880, it was re-erected as a gateway at Theobalds Park in Hertfordshire. There it remained until 2003 when it was returned to the City of London and now stands, cleaned and restored, in Paternoster Square near to St Paul's Cathedral.

Stereographs of London.

By Valentine Blanchard.

No. 516.—Temple Bar.

ST. JOHN'S GATE (OLD CITY GATE). 15

St John's Gate, c.1875

This gateway is all that remains of the Clerkenwell priory of the Order of the Hospital of St John of Jerusalem. It was built in 1504 and by the eighteenth century housed the offices of the publishers of the *Gentleman's Magazine*. Dr Samuel Johnson wrote for the magazine and, it was reported, spent more time here than in his own lodgings.

St John's Gate was preserved and restored by public subscription in 1845-46 at a time when the development of the area might have swept it away. The boy street traders with their fruit stall reminds us of the busy commercial life of Victorian London streets.

OLD HOUSES IN GRAY'S INN – THE FIELD COURT, 1878 AND GRAY'S INN LANE, 1885

In 1827, Charles Dickens began work at Gray's Inn as a clerk for Edward Blackmore, a friend of his father. John Forster maintained the job was little more than an 'office-lad'. Clearly the place was not viewed with great affection by Dickens, as in an essay in *The Uncommercial Traveller* entitled 'Chambers' he described Gray's Inn as 'one of the most depressing institutions in brick and mortar, known to the children of men'. He went on, 'Can anything be more dreary than its arid Square, Sahara Desert of the law, with the ugly old tiled-topped tenements, the dirty windows, the bills To Let, To Let, the door-posts inscribed like gravestones, the crazy gateway giving upon the filthy Lane, the scowling, iron-barred prison-like passage into Verulam-buildings . . . ' The 'Old Houses' shown opposite the entrance to Verulam Buildings, were demolished as part of a road widening scheme in 1878-9.

No. 522.—*Tomb of John Bunyan, in Bunhill Fields Cemetery.*

The tomb of John Bunyan, in Bunhill Fields Cemetery, c.1865

Bunyan's *Pilgrim's Progress* remained a popular work in Victorian Britain. Bunyan's tomb in the non-conformist burial ground, Bunhill Fields, on the northerly edge of the City of London attracted many curious visitors. Dickens was inspired by his work and *The Old Curiosity Shop* is the novel most closely aligned to Bunyan's vision. In the story, Little Nell reads *Pilgrim's Progress* and her life story can be viewed as a sort of pilgrimage as she leaves London or 'the City of Destruction'.

St. Bartholomew the Great, c.1877

By the early 19th century many of the city's churchyards were full. They remained rather desolate and unloved areas. On the left hand side of the approach to the St. Bartholomew the Great a railed and raised graveyard was visible. Dickens was drawn to such places and described them in a powerful way in his writings. In this passage from *Nicholas Nickleby*, Ralph Nickleby passed 'a poor, mean burial-ground – a dismal place, raised a few feet above the level of the street, and parted from it by a low parapet-wall and an iron railing; a rank, unwholesome, rotten spot, where the very grass and weeds seemed, in their frouzy growth, to tell that they had sprung from paupers' bodies, and had struck their roots in the graves of men, sodden, while alive, in steaming courts and drunken hungry dens. And here, in truth, they lay, parted from the living by a little earth and a board or two – lay thick and close – corrupting in body as they had in mind – a dense and squalid crowd.'

BARNARD'S INN – THE FETTER LANE FRONT, THE INNER COURTYARD, AND THE HALL, 1879, HENRY DIXON

Barnard's Inn, one of London's Inns of Chancery where lawyers trained, is situated just off Holborn. The Hall dates back to the late 15th century. The Inn features in *Great Expectations* when Pip stayed there. When he first heard its name, he supposed that it might be a tavern or public house. On arrival he described it as the 'dingiest collection of shabby buildings ever squeezed together in a rank corner as a club for Tom-cats . . . the windows of the sets of chambers into which those houses were divided were in every stage of dilapidated blind and curtain, crippled flower-pot, cracked glass, dusty decay, and miserable makeshift.'

CLIFFORD'S INN AND OLD HOUSES, FLEET STREET, 1884 & 1885

By the nineteenth century, many of the capital's newspaper and printing offices were located in Fleet Street or in the numerous alleys and courts that led off it. *The Daily News*, advertised on right-hand shop-front, was a radical newspaper that Dickens had established and briefly edited in early 1846. At the back of these houses lay Clifford's Inn, an Inn of Chancery. It could be approached via various small lanes. In the vicinity of this part of Fleet Street in *Our Mutual Friend*, Rokesmith confronts Mr Boffin and says, 'Would you object to turn aside into this place – I think it is called Clifford's Inn – where we can hear one another better than in the roaring street?' Many of the Inns of Court had small gardens which Dickens was very disparaging about. Here it was a 'mouldy little plantation or cat-preserve . . . Sparrows were there, cats were there, dry-rot and wet-rot were there, but it was not otherwise a suggestive spot.'

CHARTERHOUSE ENTRANCE, GREAT HALL, CLOISTERS, WASHHOUSE COURT C.1880, HENRY DIXON

Charterhouse is situated to the north-east of Smithfield Market. Established first as a Carthusian monastery then later as a hospital and school for 'poor brethren and scholars', by the mid nineteenth century 80 pensioners lived on the site and the school had under 200 pupils. Two of Dickens's acquaintances, the novelist William Makepeace Thackeray and the artist John Leech, were educated there. In 1855, an article in Dickens's weekly *Household Words* written by Henry Morley revealed the wide disparity between the income and the 'luxuriously fitted thirty-two roomed residence' of the Master and the poor living conditions and meagre allowance of the Charterhouse pensioners.

LINDSEY HOUSE, LINCOLN'S INN FIELDS, 1882

Lincoln's Inn Fields was laid out as a fashionable residential square in the seventeenth century. Dickens's great friend and later biographer, John Forster lived at No. 58 Lincoln's Inn Fields, the grand building to the left of Lindsey House. It was the home of the lawyer Tulkinghorn in *Bleak House*, 'Here, in a large house, formerly a house of state, lives Mr Tulkinghorn. It is let off in sets of chambers now; and in those shrunken fragments of its greatness, lawyers lie like maggots in nuts. But its roomy staircases, passages, and antechambers, still remain.'

LINCOLN'S INN OLD SQUARE, 1876

Lincoln's Inn is one of the four Inns of Court. This view shows the buildings to the north of the gatehouse. Dickens opens *Bleak House* in Lincoln's Inn Old Hall where the Court of Chancery used to meet out of legal term-times. It is used as the setting in the book for the interminable hearings associated with the case of Jarndyce and Jarndyce. An evocative passage describes the area on a summer's day out of term-time, 'like tidal harbours at low water; where stranded proceedings, offices at anchor, idle clerks lounging on lop-sided stools that will not recover their perpendicular until the current of Term sets in, lie high and dry upon the ooze of the long vacation. Outer doors of chambers are shut up by the score, messages and parcels are to be left at the Porter's Lodge by the bushel. A crop of grass would grow in the chinks of the stone pavement outside Lincoln's Inn Hall . . .'

The Mystery of Edwin Drood

'Behind the most ancient part of Holborn, where certain gabled houses, some centuries of age, still stand looking on the public way, as if disconsolately looking for the Old Bourne that has long run dry, is a little nook composed of two irregular quadrangles, called Staple Inn. It is one of those nooks, the turning into which, out of the clashing street, imparts to the relieved pedestrian the sensation of having put cotton in his ears, and velvet soles on his boots. It is one of those nooks where a few smoky sparrows twitter in smoky trees, as though they called to one another, "Let us play at country," and where a few feet of garden mould and a few yards of gravel enable them to do that refreshing violence to their tiny understandings.'

Old Houses in Holborn, c.1878

This photograph shows some houses in Holborn which still exist today but look quite different. They date from the late sixteenth century and once formed part of Staple Inn, one of the Inns of Chancery. Very badly damaged by bombing in the Second World War, they were restored in the 1950s and clad with timbering and painted black and white. In the 1870s, the upper stories of the buildings seem in a ruinous state with a number of broken windows. A policeman stands to the right of the lamppost and on the extreme right an obelisk marks the boundary of the City of London. This was where tolls were levied on wagons entering the City. In this area, an ancient row of buildings, Middle Row, was viewed as an 'obstructive eyesore of long standing'. It encroached on the highway and restricted the flow of traffic until it was finally demolished in 1867.

Canonbury Tower, 1879

This distinctive building dates back to the sixteenth century and is referred to in a Dickens story about a lamplighter who resided somewhere nearby. The author seems to have associated the Canonbury area as being 'a quiet part of town, where there were some queer old houses.' The photograph shows a street lamp directly in the front of the Tower, the type that would have been on the 'beat' or rounds of the lamplighter.

TOWER OF LONDON, C.1875

Dickens in his novel *Barnaby Rudge* describes how
Lord George Gordon, the instigator of the Gordon
Riots, was held in the Tower, 'in a dreary room
whose thick stone walls shut out the hum of life.'
In 1840, the writer William Harrison Ainsworth, a
friend of Dickens, published his popular historical
novel on the life of Lady Jane Grey calling it *The
Tower of London*.

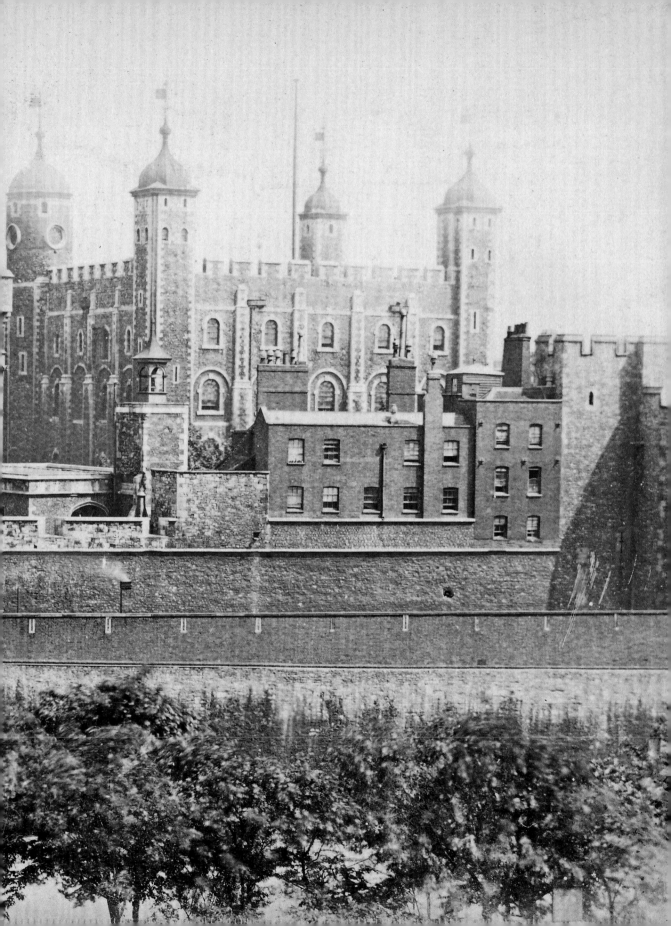

VIEW OF GREENWICH, 1856

This photograph looks down from the Royal Observatory over part of Greenwich Park, the Queen's House and the Old Royal Naval College and across to the Isle of Dogs. Dickens wrote one of his *Sketches by Boz* about the popular Easter and Whitsun Greenwich Fair. Tens of thousands of Londoners were attracted to the stalls and sideshows in the park. The fair was closed in 1857 because its unruly nature offended Victorian sensibilities. Dickens loved dining with his friends at Greenwich taverns such as the Ship, the Crown and Sceptre and the Trafalgar. Between March and September whitebait dinners were a speciality, accompanied by champagne or punch.

SLUMS

For poorer Londoners, work and housing were hard to find. Families scraped a living by sending their children out to sell fruit and vegetables in the streets. In run-down areas, single rooms and damp cellars in old houses were shared by several families. London was a city of great contrasts. The poor had to stay in the centre of town, close to their places of work and to the markets. The old city-centre housing stock that had been vacated by those moving out to the suburbs was taken on by unscrupulous landlords and middlemen. They divided up the rooms of large houses and charged high rents. In the worst cases, a single room or a damp cellar might be shared by several families. Outside, sewage flowed down the squalid alleys and courtyards. These overcrowded 'rookeries' or 'slums' (the word was first used in the early Victorian period) were considered breeding grounds of crime and depravity. Charles Dickens in his writings drew attention to such places, condemning local and national government in their lack of action in alleviating the terrible situation of the urban poor.

Londoners living in such surroundings suffered crippling diseases, but local parishes did little to relieve their suffering. It took cholera and typhus outbreaks to frighten the authorities into action. One strategy was simply to clear away the slums while carrying out road improvements. But as Karl Marx (who moved to London in 1849 and remained until his death in 1883) observed, by destroying houses such schemes hunted 'the labourer from one quarter to another' and crowded London's poor even more closely together. Child mortality was very high in nineteenth-century London. Many children lost one or more of their brothers and sisters before they were two or three years old. Disposal of the dead pressed more heavily on the poorer parishes, where graveyards became as catastrophically overcrowded as the houses occupied by the living.

The Irish formed the largest immigrant group in London. The first great wave of immigrants peaked in 1851 when 109,000 Irish-born people were recorded in the census. Many of the Irish who came to London had been driven from their homes by famine and arrived in the city already poor. Although Irish immigrants included people of all classes, education and backgrounds, the London Irish were often stereotyped as poor and feckless. In the capital their poverty was exacerbated by the areas in which they lived: Whitechapel, Southwark and the area round St Giles known as 'Little Dublin' contained some of the city's most unhealthy properties. Charles Dickens was attracted as well as appalled by such localities. He found inspiration for his writings in the people who lived and worked in such environments.

The 1834 Poor Law Amendment Act transferred the relief of the poor from the parishes to new local Boards of Guardians. This was largely the work of the civil servant Edwin Chadwick. He believed that pauperism was a contagious moral disease, whose main threat was its potential to infect the honest working man. Paupers were sent to the workhouse, where they lived, were fed and, if able-bodied, put to work picking oakum and stone-breaking in labour yards. However, some London parishes did continue to provide poor relief and give out dole. In times of economic depression, the number of vagrants and unemployed labourers in the metropolis was sometimes greater than places available in the workhouses.

Workhouses, known as Poor Law Bastilles, became notorious for the cruelties and indignities practised inside. Friedrich Engels was among many horrified by the system. 'The law in its essence proclaims the poor criminals, the workhouses prisons, their inmates beyond the pale of the law, beyond the pale of humanity, objects of disgust and repulsion', he wrote.

Previous page: **Lower Fore Street, Lambeth, c.1865**

This street close to the river Thames evokes the enclosed environment inhabited by many poor Londoners in mid nineteenth-century London. The group of children and women sit beneath an elaborate sign board promoting a local boat builder and oar and scull maker. One wonders whether these children go to school or possibly they form part of what Dickens called the 'Thirty thousand children, hunted, flogged, imprisoned, but not taught – who might have been nurtured by the wolf or the bear, so little of humanity had they, within them or without'.

The Crawlers, 1877

This famous photograph by John Thomson portrays a destitute child minder sitting on the steps of St Giles's and St George's Workhouse in Short's Gardens. Adolphe Smith described 'crawlers' as poverty-stricken individuals so poor that they were unable to work or even find the energy to beg.

YORK WHARF, UPPER FORE STREET, LAMBETH, 1866

When cholera struck the capital in the 1849, the riverside district of Lambeth was one of the worst hit. The poor used water from the heavily polluted Thames and open sewers ran down the middle of the streets and alleys.

LOWER FORE STREET (*above*) **AND UPPER FORE STREET** (*right*), C. 1865

The narrow cobblestoned streets, often no more than a cart wide, are lined with small ramshackle houses facing the brick walls and entrances of factories and potteries. Lambeth was industrial area and very densely populated. The number of inhabitants in the parish had risen from around 28,000 in 1801 to nearly 300,000 at the time this photograph was taken. Perhaps it was such localities that made Dickens write that he found London 'a vile place' with 'that great heavy canopy lowering over the housetops'. Despite the gloomy aspect, there is life here. A bird cage, probably containing a song bird, hangs from an upstairs window, windows are open and curtains flap in the wind.

THAMES FORESHORE AT
UPPER FORE STREET, LAMBETH, C.1865

These photographs by William Strudwick are the only surviving mid nineteenth-century images of a London working-class district. They show riverside premises as well as slum streets. They were taken to record the area before the building of the Albert Embankment. The area was very prone to flooding, not helped by the badly-maintained brick river walls. Up to the early nineteenth century, there were fishermen who worked here but as the river water became more polluted all the fish had died by the 1850s. This was an industrial locality dependent on barges delivering raw materials and taking away finished goods on a daily basis. Many watermen, lightermen and wharf labourers were employed along this stretch of the river. Small boat and barge yards built and repaired craft on the muddy foreshore.

VIEW LOOKING DOWN
LOWER FORE STREET, C.1865

Upper and Lower Fore Street was a long narrow thoroughfare running from St Mary's Church and Lambeth Palace in the north nearly all the way to Vauxhall Bridge in the south. On either side there were small factories, warehouses, wharves and rows of houses. Perhaps the most prominent industry in the vicinity was salt-glaze stoneware manufacturing. Some of the potteries had become substantial operations such as that of Henry Doulton's at the northern end and James Stiff's further south, partly seen here. They made domestic wares such as jugs and pots as well as drain and sewage pipes. Most of the potteries had their main entrances fronting Lambeth High Street. In this view, an overhead walkway connects Stiff's premises on either side of Fore Street, with the building on the right fronting directly on to the river Thames.

Street Floods in Lambeth, John Thomson, 1877

John Thomson, the photographer, explained that his image revealed something of the unfortunate lives of the Lambeth poor. The woman on the left, Mrs Rowlett, related that the 'water has taken us down a bit, and the last midnight flood was too much for my old man. He now has severe congestion of the lungs'. The central woman carrying her child in her arms, lived in an adjoining house with her husband. They were 'country folk tempted into town by the hope of higher wages'. The figure on the right was quite a local character, known as a comedian in the taverns and by day a 'beach-picker' or 'mudlark' who scoured the foreshore for things that could be sold. During the floods he had become an 'odd handy man' helping those affected by the invading water.

The old dry dock in Stangate, Lambeth, c.1865

The locality of Lambeth features in a number of Dickens's novels and stories. It is where the evil Squeers in *Nicholas Nickleby* takes lodgings when he comes down to London. In one of the essays from *Household Words*, 'Three Detective Anecdotes', a glove-cleaner tells how he had been dining at Lambeth at a free-and-easy (a public house where customers joined in sing-songs as they drank and ate) describing it as 'quite promiscuous'. In the evenings, Dickens visited sometimes the Bower Saloon in Stangate, a small theatre attached to the Duke's Tavern, known for its melodramas and often rather rowdy audiences.

Broad Street, Lambeth, c.1865

In the distance, barges can distinguished on the Thames with the wharves and factory chimneys across the river at Millbank. It is high tide and the river water is flowing up the street. As a particularly low-lying area, Lambeth was subject to frequent flooding. This was one of the main reasons why the area was swept away when the Albert Embankment was built between 1866 and 1869. Barges delivered supplies to Crowley's Alton Ale wharf, one of the main depots for an ale that was brewed in Hampshire and had become very popular in London in the Victorian period. Alton Ale stores offered a pint of ale and sandwich for a very cheap price. Dickens mentioned a 'feeding place' that offered 'a first-rate sandwich and sparkling glass of Alton Ale for threepence'.

OLD HOUSES AND SHOPS IN STANGATE, LAMBETH, C.1865

These buildings were situated close to the southern approaches to Westminster Bridge and just near the back entrance into Astley's Amphitheatre. The Bower Saloon and Canterbury Theatre were also nearby. The wall outside the small tobacconist shop is smothered with newspaper adverts. At the door of an even smaller shop to the left stands a girl with a rolling hoop. This area was cleared and St Thomas's Hospital was built on the site.

FROM

Bleak House

'I T IS A BLACK, dilapidated street, avoided by all decent people, where the crazy houses were seized upon, when their decay was far advanced, by some bold vagrants who after establishing their own possession took to letting them out in lodgings. Now, these tumbling tenements contain, by night, a swarm of misery . . . Twice lately there has been a crash and a cloud of dust, like the springing of a mine, in Tom-all-Alone's; and each time a house has fallen. These accidents have made a paragraph in the newspapers and have filled a bed or two in the nearest hospital. The gaps remain, and there are not unpopular lodgings among the rubbish. As several more houses are nearly ready to go, the next crash in Tom-all-Alone's may be expected to be a good one.'

THE ONE TUN RAGGED SCHOOL, PERKINS RENTS, C.1870

In 1853, a ragged school opened in a part of Westminster, close to the Houses of Parliament, popularly known as the 'Devil's Acre'. It was a very poor slum area and Dickens wrote of it as 'an awful place . . . a maze of filth and squalor' and its inhabitants as 'very low and wretched'. The philanthropist Adeline M Cooper raised money to convert an empty public house into a ragged school. The One Tun's landlord had stripped the premises before he left without paying the rent. By 1871, the school had an average attendance of 133 pupils. Adeline Cooper also set up the Duck Lane Working Man's Club nearby. Adeline Cooper was described in Dickens's magazine *All the Year Round* as 'a lady who estimates as the highest privilege of her wealth the means of doing good'.

THE OLD CLOTHES OF ST GILES, 1877

This shop is in Lumber Court. A report into charities in London showed that a number of houses in Lumber Court belonged to Miss E Palmer's charity. They were old and in bad condition and let out to unscrupulous landlords who maximised rental returns and skimped on maintenance. Photographer Adolphe Smith noted that 'it was here that the poorest inhabitants of a district renowned for its poverty, both buy and sell their clothes… Few persons have a better insight into the hard side of life than the dealers in old clothes; for it is to them that are brought the apparel which has been rejected by the pawnbrokers as unsuitable guarantee for even the smallest loan'. Of St Giles, Dickens's description picked out especially the 'sickening smells, these heaps of filth, these tumbling houses with all their vile contents, animate and inaminate'. Despite the area's poverty, he loved to stroll along Monmouth Street which was full of old clothes retailers. He called it the 'burial-place of the fashions'.

Sketches by Boz

'THERE ARE CERTAIN descriptions of people who, oddly enough, appear to appertain exclusively to the metropolis. You meet them, every day, in the streets of London, but no one ever encounters them elsewhere; they seem indigenous to the soil, and to belong as exclusively to London as its own smoke, or the dingy bricks and mortar. We could illustrate the remark by a variety of examples, but, in our present sketch, we will only advert to one class as a specimen – that class which is so aptly and expressively designated as 'shabby-genteel'.

Now, shabby people, God knows, may be found anywhere, and genteel people are not articles of greater scarcity out of London than in it; but this compound of the two – this shabby-gentility – is as purely local as the statue at Charing-cross, or the pump at Aldgate. It is worthy of remark, too, that only men are shabby-genteel; a woman is always either dirty and slovenly in the extreme, or neat and respectable, however poverty-stricken in appearance. A very poor man, 'who has seen better days,' as the phrase goes, is a strange compound of dirty-slovenliness and wretched attempts at faded smartness . . . If you meet a man, lounging up Drury-Lane, or leaning with his back against a post in Long-acre, with his hands in the pockets of a pair of drab trousers plentifully besprinkled with grease-spots: the trousers made very full over the boots, and ornamented with two cords down the outside of each leg – wearing, also, what has been a brown coat with bright buttons, and a hat very much pinched up at the side, cocked over his right eye – don't pity him. He is not shabby-genteel. The "harmonic meetings" at some fourth-rate public-house, or the purlieus of a private theatre, are his chosen haunts; he entertains a rooted antipathy to any kind of work, and is on familiar terms with several pantomime men at the large houses. But, if you see hurrying along a by-street, keeping as close as he can to the area-railings, a man of about forty or fifty, clad in an old rusty suit of threadbare black cloth which shines with constant wear as if it had been bees-waxed – the trousers tightly strapped down, partly for the look of the thing and partly to keep his old shoes from slipping off at the heels, – if you observe, too, that his yellowish-white neckerchief is carefully pinned up, to conceal the tattered garment underneath, and that his hands are encased in the remains of an old pair of beaver gloves, you may set him down as a shabby-genteel man. A glance at that depressed face, and timorous air of conscious poverty, will make your heart ache – always supposing that you are neither a philosopher nor a political economist.'

CLARE MARKET, C.1890

In the early nineteenth century this market, situated at the south-west corner of Lincoln's Inn Fields, sold meat, fish and fresh vegetables. There were many taverns in the vicinity. Joe Grimaldi, the famous clown, was born in Stanhope Street adjoining the market. Dickens alluded to the area as a place that had 'houses of a poor description, swarming with inhabitants'. This 'rookery' or slum quarter was swept away at the start of the twentieth century forming part of the Aldwych and Kingsway improvement scheme.

COACHING INNS
AND HORSE-DRAWN TRANSPORT

Stagecoaches departed from London's principal coaching inns at all times of the day. Dickens described an early morning scene at one of them in *Sketches by Boz* with passengers gathering in the travellers' room. It was usually necessary to book in advance for the more popular routes as the largest coaches could carry only a maximum of twelve passengers. Coaching proprietors operated both long-distance and short-stage services. The system was efficient but stagecoaches were slow and often uncomfortable. A journey from London to Birmingham took at least fourteen hours. When the railways arrived the same journey was cut to only five and half hours. In the early 1830s though, each day, hundreds of long-stage coaches arrived and departed, carrying passengers, small packages and the Royal Mail between the metropolis and virtually every town and village in the country.

Coaching inns lined all of the main thoroughfares of the city. On the same routes, teams of horses drew large, wide-wheeled wagons, laden with manufactured goods and materials. Heavy produce normally arrived in London by coastal sailing craft or canal barge, though its final destination could be quite some distance from the water's edge. The metropolis supported a vast number of coach builders and horse equipment manufacturers, who supplied the transport industry with everything from wheels and axles to reins and whips. The streets of London were filled with the clatter and smell of horse-drawn vehicles.

At the time that Dickens was publishing his first novels, William Chaplin was London's principal proprietor of stage and mail coaches. He operated over one hundred of them out of three coaching inns. A shrewd businessman, Chaplin survived the decline of the stagecoach by becoming an omnibus proprietor. He also negotiated a contract with the London and Birmingham Railway to transport freight from the terminus into the city centre. The coaching inns were also the depots for fly wagons which transported goods to provincial cities and villages and towns along the way. They moved continuously through the capital, day and night. This highly-organised road haulage system provided a vital link between the regional economies and the commercial centre of London. The wagons could carry loads weighing up to six tons but the pace was slow. A journey between London and Exeter could take more than four days.

Toll bars and gates were positioned at the entrance to all roads maintained by turnpike trusts around London. The trusts were licensed to collect tolls from vehicles passing through their toll gates. The system generated the necessary funds for improving the condition of the roads and enabled faster and more reliable travel. A gatekeeper manned each one and was responsible for collecting tolls. Only mail coaches were exempt from payment. Certain tolls were charged by weight and vehicles had to pass over weighing-machines at the gate. Tolls were resented by drivers who often attempted to avoid payment by driving their vehicles at speed through the gates. By the 1830s more than three hundred stagecoaches provided daily services from London whilst every week over a thousand goods wagons passed in and out of the capital.

With the coming of the railways the coaching inns fell into partial disuse. Some were used as receiving houses for packages and parcels for the railway. Carts and wagons moved back and forth from the inns to the railway depots. Coach and wagon services inevitably declined as the railways extended their networks, but the demise was often regretted. In 1838, the Duke of Wellington complained that 'these accursed railways' had 'totally destroyed our convenient communications' and 'even deranged' the post.

The
Pickwick Papers

'THERE ARE in London several old inns, once the head-quarters of celebrated coaches in the days when coaches performed their journeys in a graver and more solemn manner than they do in these times; but which have now degenerated into little more than the abiding and booking-places of country wagons. The reader would look in vain for any of these ancient hostelries, among the Golden Crosses and Bull and Mouths, which rear their stately fronts in the improved streets of London. If he would light upon any of these old places, he must direct his steps to the obscurer quarters of the town, and there in some secluded nooks he will find several, still standing with a kind of gloomy sturdiness, amidst the modern innovations which surround them.'

THE OXFORD ARMS, c.1875

It was the imminent demolition of The Oxford Arms in Warwick Lane near Newgate and the Old Bailey which led to the formation of the Society for Photographing Relics of Old London in 1875. It aimed to preserve a record of parts of London which were rapidly disappearing. This sequence of photographs, taken by Alfred and John Bool and printed by Henry Dixon and Sons, illustrate a typical galleried London coaching inn. Such premises were becoming a rarity by this date. Many had fallen into decay, such as this one, as the railways took over the transportation of goods and people between towns and cities in England. From 1868 parts of The Oxford Arms were converted into tenements. Staircases, galleries, the yard and the entrance to the inn from Warwick Lane, Paternoster Row, clearly show its functions from a time when a team of horses might be drawing a wagon through the narrow gateway. The inn was demolished in 1876.

The Old Bell, Holborn, 1884

By this date, The Old Bell in Holborn, opposite Fetter Lane, was one of the last remaining coaching inns in London. Characteristic features are evident: the entrance archway leading from a potentially busy road into a yard surrounded by galleried accommodation. In his accompanying account of 1884, Alfred Marks describes that a daily omnibus departed from the inn to Uxbridge, Chalfont, Amersham and Wendover. In its heyday, other destinations would have been on offer from The Old Bell to Brighton and Cambridge as well as into Oxfordshire and Gloucestershire.

Returning from the Derby, c.1860

It seemed as if the whole of fashionable Victorian London society left the capital in early June each year for Epsom on the day of the Derby. This coloured stereo card captures some of the revelry as groups of Londoners return to town after the race. Dickens and W H Wills wrote a joint essay entitled 'Epsom' for *Household Words* where they described the array of vehicles arriving at Epsom: 'Then came flitting by, barouches, phaetons, broughams, gigs, four-wheeled chaises, four-in-hands, Hansom cabs, cabs of lesser note, chaise-carts, donkey-carts, tilted vans made arbourescent with green boughs carrying no end of people, and a cask of beer – '. The return was just as dramatic and attracted thousands of spectators along the route back to London: 'So now we are on the road again, going home . . . for we are a dense mass of men and women, wheels, horses and dust. Now, all the houses on the road seem to be turned inside out, like the carriages on the course, and the people belonging to the houses, like people belonging to the carriages, occupy stations which they never occupy at another time; on leads, on housetops, on out-buildings, at windows, in balconies, in doorways, in gardens . . . The crowd thickens on both sides of the road. London seems to have come out to see us.'

Flying Dustmen, 1877

In *Bleak House*, a dustman is called in twice to carry off 'a cart load of old paper, ashes, and broken bottles' from Krook's rag and bottle shop after his death.

The Water Cart, 1877

In the summer months, London streets became very dry and dusty. Horse-drawn carts with special metal water tanks hosed the main thoroughfares, turning the dust on the ground into mud.

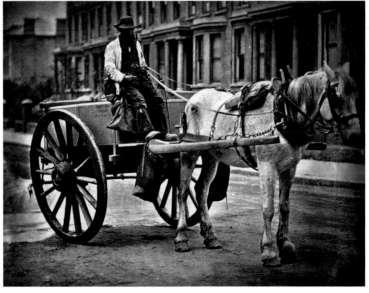

The Coaching Inns of Southwark

In the early nineteenth century, Borough High Street was an extremely important route in and out of London, with four coaches a day going to Maidstone, two to Dover and Canterbury, and one to Brighton and Hastings. A number of inns along the street provided rest for travellers and a place where horses were changed before coaches continued on their journey either to the south or the north. When the capital only had one river crossing – London Bridge – the inns were the principal southern termini for coaches arriving and departing the capital. By the 1820s, however, London had six bridges and many coaches passed through Southwark into the central district of the city. The inns there were more convenient than those in Borough High Street. Dickens would have travelled this way from Chatham in 1822 before crossing the river and arriving at The Cross Keys in Wood Street, Cheapside.

FROM

The Pickwick Papers

———— ❧ ————

'In the Borough especially, there still remain some half-dozen old inns, which have preserved their external features unchanged, and which have escaped alike the rage for public improvement and the encroachments of private speculation. Great, rambling queer old places they are, with galleries, and passages, and staircases, wide enough and antiquated enough to furnish materials for a hundred ghost stories, supposing we should ever be reduced to the lamentable necessity of inventing any, and that the world should exist long enough to exhaust the innumerable veracious legends connected with old London Bridge, and its adjacent neighbourhood on the Surrey side.'

Queen's Head Inn, c.1881

John Harvard, the benefactor of Harvard College, Cambridge, Massachusetts, owned the Queen's Head for a short time in the seventeenth century. The inn survived the Southwark fire of 1676. When the main building of the Queen's Head was taken down in 1856, the timber was discovered to date from Tudor times. The rest of the inn was demolished in 1900.

The Pickwick Papers

'It was in the yard of one of these inns – of no less celebrated a one than the White Hart – that a man was busily employed in brushing the dirt off a pair of boots, early on the morning succeeding the events narrated in the last chapter. He was habited in a coarse, striped waistcoat, with black calico sleeves, and blue glass buttons; drab breeches and leggings. A bright red handkerchief was wound in a very loose and unstudied style round his neck, and an old white hat was carelessly thrown on one side of his head. There were two rows of boots before him, one cleaned and the other dirty, and at every addition he made to the clean row, he paused from his work, and contemplated its results with evident satisfaction.

The yard presented none of that bustle and activity which are the usual characteristics of a large coach inn. Three or four lumbering wagons, each with a pile of goods beneath its ample canopy, about the height of the second-floor window of an ordinary house, were stowed away beneath a lofty roof which extended over one end of the yard; and another, which was probably to commence its journey that morning, was drawn out into the open space. A double tier of bedroom galleries, with old clumsy balustrades, ran round two sides of the straggling area, and a double row of bells to correspond, sheltered from the weather by a little sloping roof, hung over the door leading to the bar and coffee-room. Two or three gigs and chaise-carts were wheeled up under different little sheds and pent-houses; and the occasional heavy tread of a cart-horse, or rattling of a chain at the farther end of the yard, announced to anybody who cared about the matter, that the stable lay in that direction. When we add that a few boys in smock-frocks were lying asleep on heavy packages, wool-packs, and other articles that were scattered about on heaps of straw, we have described as fully as need be the general appearance of the yard of the White Hart Inn, High Street, Borough, on the particular morning in question.'

Previous page and above: **THE WHITE HART INN, C.1881**

This is the famous inn associated with Samuel Weller and Dickens's novel *The Pickwick Papers*. Henry Dixon's photographs show the place in a state of sad decline from its former greatness as one of Southwark's main coaching inns. However, the large extent of the property shows how important it must have been in previous years. As trade diminished, parts of the site were converted into tenements or local industrial use. The White Hart Inn was finally demolished in 1889.

GEORGE INN YARD, C.1881

This image by Henry Dixon shows the only part of the George Inn that survives to the present day. The inn's large courtyard was being used as a railway goods depot when the photograph was taken.

KING'S HEAD INN YARD, C.1881

The inn was originally called the Pope's Head but changed its name at the time of the Reformation. John Taylor in his *Carriers' Cosmographie* of 1637 noted that the 'carriers from Chittington, Westrum, Penborough, Slenge, Wrotham, and other parts of Kent, Sussex, and Surrey, do lodge at the *King's Head* in Southwark [and]. . . do come on Thursdays, and they go on Fridays'. This photograph still gives a sense of a working inn, with stabling for horses. The inn had been completely demolished by 1889.

MARKETS AND STREET LIFE

Feeding London's enormous and rapidly-expanding population became a major problem during the first half of the nineteenth century. Most of the capital's food markets had difficulty coping with the enormous quantities of fresh produce and live animals arriving each day. In 1828 an Act for regulating Covent Garden led to the construction of a new covered marketplace for fruit and vegetables, designed by Charles Fowler. The rival Hungerford Market was also rebuilt by Fowler in the early 1830s. The blacking factory where Dickens had worked was demolished as part of its construction. In *Sketches by Boz*, there is a description of the early morning as market produce arrives in the metropolis:

> '*Market-carts roll slowly along: the sleepy waggoner impatiently urging on his tired horses, or vainly endeavouring to awaken the boy, who, luxuriously stretched on the top of the fruit-baskets, forgets, in happy oblivion, his long-cherished curiosity to behold the wonders of London . . . Numbers of men and women (principally the latter), carrying upon their heads heavy baskets of fruit, toil down the park side of Piccadilly, on their way to Covent-garden, and, following each other in rapid succession, form a long straggling line from thence to the turn of the road at Knightsbridge.*'

In 1850, the City Corporation instructed its architect, James Bunning, to draw up plans to replace the old dock and fish market at Billingsgate. The dock was filled in and a new market building constructed on the site overlooking the Thames. The new market opened in 1852 but the facilities were soon found to be insufficient for the amount of fish handled and sold each day. In 1877, the market was enlarged to the designs of Sir Horace Jones. It was reported that in the vicinity of London Bridge and the Monument, it was possible to smell your way to Billingsgate. Vast quantities of fish were delivered each day by small fishing smacks to the dock at Billingsgate. Further fish came overland to the market. Live eels transported by Dutch eel *schuyts* or boats were becoming less prevalent. This was due to the polluted state of the river Thames. Many eels were poisoned and died as the river water flowed through the wells in the bottom of the Dutch vessels.

Smithfield Market, in particular, attracted the attention of reformers. The streets in the area were often impassable, blocked by thousands of cattle and sheep on the way to market. The stench and noise from the nearby slaughterhouses was terrible. No improvements were made until 1855 when the livestock market was re-sited to a large new facility at Copenhagen fields, Islington. This was a more regulated market than the old one at Smithfield. Although the railways were used to transport livestock there, drovers still brought large herds of cattle and flocks of sheep by road. Cattle drovers had to wear special numbered arm badges in London, carrying the Corporation of London's coat of arms.

Throughout Victorian London, vast numbers of street traders operated selling all types of goods. Sometimes their wares were set out on costermonger barrows in established street markets. Others just walked the streets carrying baskets or sat on the pavements encouraging those passing to buy their goods. Social reformer Henry Mayhew, in his book *London Labour and the London Poor* attempted to survey all the different street traders. He wrote,

> '*Those who obtain their living in the streets of the metropolis are a very large and varied class; indeed, the means resorted to in order "to pick up a crust", as the people call it, in the public thoroughfares (and such in many instances it literally is,) are so multifarious that the mind is long baffled in its attempts to reduce them to scientific order or classification.*'

Previous page: **THE CHEAP FISH OF ST GILES'S, 1877**

This photograph shows Joseph Carney, a costermonger, selling
fresh herring from a barrow in a street market in the vicinity
of the Seven Dials. The boy with the white pitcher on the right,
known locally as 'Little Mic-Mac Gosling', was 17 years old
though only three feet ten inches (1.16 metres) high.

SMITHFIELD MEAT MARKET 19

SMITHFIELD MEAT MARKET, C.1878

The Smithfield Central Market building, designed by Sir Horace Jones, the Corporation of London's chief architect, was completed in 1868. The regularity of the scene, with the rows of carts lined up waiting to take away the carcasses of meat, was very different to what Dickens had viewed in the 1850s when he campaigned for the closure of the old livestock market and the surrounding slaughterhouses.

PUNCH AND JUDY SHOW, C.1865

This street Punch and Judy show is being held in Waterloo Place with the Crimean War Memorial visible in the background. Dickens defended such popular street entertainment as being harmless in its influence and an extravagant relief 'from the realities of life which would lose its hold upon the people if it were made moral and instructive'.

THE LONDON BOARDMEN, 1877

Dickens described this type of street advertiser as 'an animated sandwich, composed of a boy between two boards'. The term 'sandwich men' thus came into common use. Adolphe Smith noted in 1877 how 'the old joke, the query as to the whereabouts of the mustard' had 'died out'. In this photograph, the boardman or 'walking advertiser' is promoting Renovo, a patented fabric cleaner.

COVENT GARDEN FLOWER WOMEN, 1877

Dickens often wore a flower fastened to his jacket's buttonhole. His favourite flower was a red geranium which he usually sported when giving his public readings. There were many flower sellers and florists in the vicinity of Covent Garden Market. Here, three flower sellers are standing in front of St. Paul's Church on the west side of the market.

COVENT GARDEN LABOURERS, 1877

Covent Garden Market held a special fascination for Charles Dickens. He had visited the area as a boy during his breaks when he was working at the blacking factory, remarking how he 'stared at the pine-apples'. This photograph shows some flower porters and salesmen who worked for Thomas Dickson, a florist with premises in the central alley at Covent Garden Market.

COVENT GARDEN MARKET, VALENTINE BLANCHARD C. 1860

In the 1860s, Charles Dickens had a private apartment on the third floor of 26 Wellington Street, above the offices of his periodical *All the Year Round*. Known as his 'temporary Town Tent', it was very close to Covent Garden Market.

DEALER IN FANCYWARE, JOHN THOMSON, 1877

Dickens in his 1865 Christmas story 'Doctor Marigold's Prescriptions', published in *All the Year Round*, has as its main character a 'Cheap Jack', a travelling salesman and pedlar who dealt in goods from the back of a cart at selected 'pitches' in different areas of the city. Fancyware dealers sold items such as watches and chronometers, rolling pins, crockery and glass items. Like most street traders, they were known for their sales patter which drew in those passing in the street.

The Seller of Shellfish, 1877

A whelk seller has used a drape to shade his stall. Such barrows were located close to public houses and the theatres. A good trade existed especially amongst poor Londoners for such street food.

Halfpenny Ices, 1877

Italians dominated the ice-cream trade on London's streets. Many lived in the Saffron Hill district where Dickens had sited Fagin's thieves' den in *Oliver Twist*.

A Convict's Home, 1877

James Baylis stands outside his dining rooms in Drury Lane. He was known for taking in 'ticket-of-leave' men after they had left prison. No released prisoners are shown in the photograph but Ramo Sammy, a well known Indian street musician who played a 'tam-tam' or metal gong stands to his right. Baylis had previously been a policeman. He knew Charles Dickens and had shown him the Adelphi Arches and explained 'all the mysteries of this notorious resort'.

Street Advertising, 1877

Charles Dickens wrote an essay called 'Bill-Sticking' where he described how disused buildings in London were 'thickly encrusted with fragments of bills'. He noted some of the most prolific advertisers of the metropolis including Madame Tussaud, the cheap clothing retailer Moses and Son, and Professor Holloway and Cabburn, both patent medicine makers. It was also a period when advertising posters were increasing in size from to 'two sheet double-crown' to 'four-sheet bills' which resulted in 'bill-stickers' having to work in pairs.

Street Doctors, John Thomson, 1877

Behind this street vendor of cough tablets, a poster advertises 'Poor Jo', a play based on Dickens's crossing sweeper in *Bleak House*. Many of Dickens's fictional characters suffered from coughs. Mr Chuffey in *Martin Chuzzlewit* explained how Jonas bought and mixed the medicine for his father's cough.

'Caney' the Clown, 1877

Life was uncertain in Victorian London. A serious illness often resulted in the loss of your job. Caney had worked as a clown for many years when a varicose vein burst while he was performing and his stage career was over. For many the only resort was to make a living on the streets. Caney's trade was repairing cane-bottom chairs.

The 'Wall Worker', 1877

These old men having a welcome drink and smoke at a tavern are 'wall workers'. Their employment consisted of, in the morning, placing wooden boards covered with adverts along fences or walls and then at night taking them down for safety. This was a fairly poorly-paid trade, usually an occupation taken on by those who had fallen on hard times.

THE DRAMATIC SHOEBLACK, 1877

Jacobus Parker, a one-time dramatic reader, stands at his 'pitch' where he works as a shoeblack and pedler. Street tradesmen would go to any lengths to make themselves stand out from their competitors. Parker displays a card with a notice from the *Parochial Critic* which explained how he had once earned a living by reciting sections of Shakespeare's plays. He was rescued from the workhouse by William Gladstone who secured for him 'a grant of £10 from the Queen's Bounty'.

THE INDEPENDENT SHOEBLACK, 1877

Dickens suggested that children could easily become 'a little robber or a vagabond' if left to roam the streets of London. Such thoughts fuelled his concern for dispossessed and unprotected children which was evident in his writings and his support of charities such as the Shoeblack Society that had been founded by Lord Shaftesbury. This shoeblack has not joined one of the nine shoeblack brigades preferring the freedom to select his own 'pitch'.

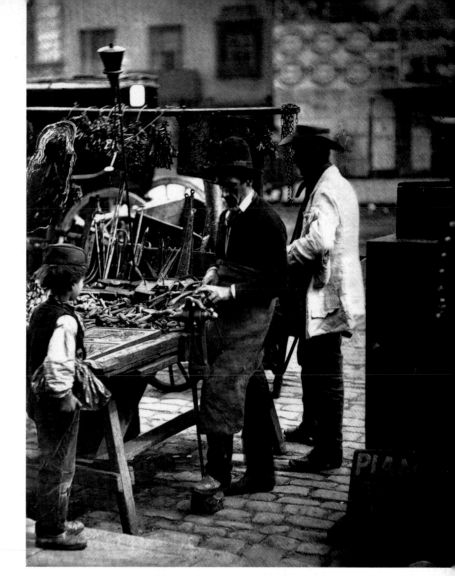

OLD FURNITURE, 1877

This photograph of a second-hand furniture dealer in Church Lane, Holborn, gives one idea of the appearance of what were termed 'marine' or broker's shops with goods spilling out on to the pavement and side of the road. Dickens writes how his 'readers must often have observed in some by-street, in a poor neighbourhood, a small dirty shop . . . In front of the shop-window, are ranged some half-dozen high-backed chairs, with spinal complaints and wasted legs; a corner cupboard; two or three very dark mahogany tables with flaps like mathematical problems'. Nicholas Nickleby, when he departed from London, settled with 'the broker from whom he had hired his poor furniture'.

THE STREET LOCKSMITH, JOHN THOMSON, 1877

Small temporary workshops were set up on many London street corners. Here, outside in Whitechapel, a locksmith works at his bench, probably filing the teeth of key held in a vice. Gabriel Varden, the locksmith in *Barnaby Rudge*, had his own workshop at the Golden Key in Clerkenwell. Dickens described the sound that the locksmith made, 'Tink, tink, tink – clear as a silver bell, and audible at every pause of the streets' harsher noises, as though it said, "I don't care; nothing puts me out; I am resolved to be happy".'

DOCKS AND THE RIVER THAMES

London was the world's largest and busiest port throughout the nineteenth century. Many visitors arrived by ship and were astonished by its appearance. Engels described the

> *'masses of buildings, the wharves on both sides*
> *. . . the countless ships along both shores, crowding*
> *ever closer and closer together, until, at last,*
> *only a narrow passage remains in the middle of*
> *the river, a passage through which hundreds of*
> *steamers shoot by one another; all this is so vast, so*
> *impressive, that a man cannot collect himself, but*
> *is lost in the marvel of England's greatness before*
> *he sets foot upon English soil.'*

It was a period of free trade and the main dock companies on the north side of the river, from west to east, the St Katharine, the London, the West India and the East India Docks entered into a period of fierce competition for the handling of the port's overseas trade. This resulted in a consolidation of the port's operation with the merger in 1838 of the East and the West India Dock Company. Prime warehouse space in the City was acquired by the three large dock companies when the East India Company sold off its City warehouses after its trade monopoly with India and the Far East was terminated. The St Katharine Dock Company secured the most prestigious one – the Cutler Street warehouses.

The other dock companies in the port were less prone to such severe competition. The Regent's Canal Dock, with its canal extending through north and west London, lined with wharves, and linking up with Grand Junction Canal at Paddington, had its own special niche market in the port. Fuel, aggregates and building materials were discharged there and distributed across London by canal.

The dock system on the south side of the river at Rotherhithe was made up of three separate companies, the Commercial, the East Country and the Surrey Canal and Dock Company. The ships that used their docks traded mainly with the Baltic region, the principal cargo being timber. The dock companies on the north bank of the river found them an annoyance, particularly the Commercial Dock Company, which had built a number of substantial warehouses around its dock, hoping to attract the North American trade. In 1864, the companies merged to form the Surrey Commercial Dock Company.

When ocean-going paddle steamships began to be introduced in the 1830s, some of the dock companies found that their lock entrances were too small for the largest ships. At first, the problem was ignored but gradually, as steamships became more established, new lock entrances were built.

The Victoria (London) Dock was London's first large dock of the industrial age. Built by the leading railway contractors, Peto, Brassey and Betts, and designed by the railway engineer George Parker Bidder, it was planned on a massive scale, with a land and water area of about two hundred acres. Its opening in 1855 led to a further series of amalgamations, as competition continued to intensify.

The private wharves along the river offered merchants very cheap storage. These wharves specialised in the handling of fresh produce such as fruit, eggs and bacon, which arrived from coastal and continental ports before being distributed to the markets and wholesalers. A number of the larger wharf companies, such as those at Hay's Wharf and Butler's Wharf, invested in constructing modern warehouses in which to store bonded goods such as wines, spirits and tea, providing blending, bottling and packaging facilities rivalling those of the dock companies. Along the Rotherhithe and Bermondsey riverfront, there were also numerous granaries which had been built or converted after the repeal of the Corn Law in 1846. These stored large quantities of foreign grain and flour, especially that from Russia and North America.

VIEW OF WESTMINSTER FROM WATERLOO BRIDGE, 1841

This photograph by William Henry Fox Talbot is thought to be the earliest photograph of the river Thames. Taken many years before the embankment was built, it shows the temporary nature of the steamboat piers with long gangplanks running across the muddy foreshore at low tide. Looking at the way in which the river bends, the photograph seems to have been taken from Waterloo Bridge before the construction of Hungerford Bridge had begun.

Previous page: MILLWALL DOCK ENTRANCE, 1867

This photograph shows the enormous entrance lock gates of the Millwall Dock before it opened in 1868. The new dock was built on land to the south of the West India Dock with a single entrance into the Thames on the western side of the Isle of Dogs at Millwall, opposite the South Dock entrance of the Surrey Commercial Dock. Kelk and Aird were the contractors of the dock and Sir Robert Fowler and William Wilson the engineers.

HUNGERFORD BRIDGE, 1845

This salt print by William Henry Fox Talbot records the new Hungerford Suspension Bridge, designed by Isambard Kingdom Brunel. The pedestrian crossing gave Londoners living on the south side of the river a more direct route to the shops, businesses and attractions of the West End as well as the Hungerford Market. The shot tower of Thomas Malthy & Co. on the south bank can be seen between the two bridge towers. The photograph was taken at the level of the foreshore close to where Northumberland and Craven Streets ran down to the river. The vicinity was described in 'Scotland Yard', one of Dickens's *Sketches by Boz*, and Craven Street was where Mr Brownlow in *Oliver Twist* lived. It is also close to where, as a boy, Dickens worked in Warren's blacking factory.

Previous page: CUSTOM HOUSE FROM THE RIVER, C.1875

On the left hand side, part of Bunning's Billingsgate Market is visible
with the tower of the Coal Exchange beyond. The steam crane and
waste shoots on the wharf probably relate to the demolition of the
old building and the construction of the new market. The Custom
House is the City of London's finest surviving early nineteenth-century
building.

SHADWELL PIERHEAD, LONDON DOCKS, 1879

These two photographs show the second Shadwell entrance lock at the eastern end of the London Dock. Built between 1854 and 1858, it allowed larger ships to enter the dock. The church spire in the view looking west is that of St. Paul's Church, Shadwell. Beyond the pierhead looking up river, a mass of lighters and sailing barges can be seen as well as a steam tug.

PHOTOGRAPHS OF THE SURREY COMMERCIAL DOCKS, 1876

These views by Morgan & Laing of Greenwich are from a series taken of the Surrey Commercial Docks around 1876. They are likely to have been commissioned by the dock company to mark newly-completed works. Relatively few photographs of London's docks exist from the mid-Victorian period. These are some of the finest that have survived. In a few of the images, the photographers have overlaid a dramatic cloud formation on to the dock scenes.

Left: **NORWAY DOCK**

This photograph, from a high vantage point, looks across to Lady Dock and Acorn Pond, and beyond to the left Russia Dock with its timber sheds. Timber was stored in the open, under cover or floating in shallow ponds. The dock company provided for the best facilities for seasoning the timber over a period of time. In the far distance, ships can be made out, on the river.

Above: **SURREY COMMERCIAL DOCK COMPANY DIRECTORS**

They stand proudly before the camera. All but one of the directors have taken off their top hats. A few curious bargees and labourers look on from a Thames sailing barge in the background.

Canada Dock, 1875-6

These photographs show the immense scale of the new 16-acre dock to the west of the Greenland Dock and south of the Acorn Dock, part of the Surrey Commercial Dock system on the south side of the river Thames. A railway track has been laid on the floor of the dock to facilitate the rapid movement of spoil and building materials across the construction site. The main contractor of the Canada dock was Thomas Docwra & Sons of Balls Pond Road, Islington. The individuals are unidentified but perhaps include one of the directors, the dock engineer and the chief foreman, admiring the dock walls before the water is let in.

GREENLAND DOCK

This was the largest and oldest cargo handling dock in the Surrey Commercial complex. Dating back to the late seventeenth century, it had first being called the Great Howland Dock but had gained a new name by the mid eighteenth century as a result of its links with London's Greenland whale fishery trade. Whale ships moored here and the boiling of whale blubber at tryworks along the south quayside of the dock would have given the dock its distinctive smell if not appearance. In this evocative photograph, a line of sailing ships are berthed along the north side of the dock, with granaries along the quayside.

SURREY LOCK

The two canal 'monkey' boats in the foreground
reveal another distinctive feature of the Surrey
Commercial Docks. A canal ran from here across
the docks and ponds in the area and then on south
to Peckham and Camberwell. Along its course, there
were many wharves and factories that were supplied
with goods by sailing barges and canal boats such
as these two. Enormous stacks of timber are evident
on the south side of the lock. In the distance, the
view is across the river towards Shadwell. Dock
labourers, foremen, lock keepers and policemen
have congregated around the entrance lock to be
part of the photograph.

SOUTH DOCK

This photograph's viewpoint has been carefully set
up. The loophole doors of the warehouse on the
south side of the dock are open and bags are being
hoisted from the quayside with dockers standing
ready on the different floors to take in the cargo.
A sailor can be seen up the mast of the innermost
sailing ship. A rope, held by a man standing in a
ship's boat, extends to a sailor leaning forward at
the stern of the outermost ship. The dock water is
very still. In the foreground, by the lock entrance,
two well-dressed men, probably dock directors, are
leaning on the lock capstan, with a small white dog
on top of it.

BLACK EAGLE WHARF, WAPPING C.1860

There are relatively few mid-Victorian photographs of London's riverside wharves. The reason for this is unclear. Perhaps this part of the river was not seen as picturesque and therefore an unsuitable subject for photographers. The constant movement of the ships and small craft in the river, even when moored, would have blurred the image. Portraits of ships were taken but this was usually carried out in the lower reaches of the river, close Gravesend, against the neutral backdrop of fields and marshland. This view captures all the variety of the Wapping riverside. The home port of the schooner, the *Express* of Alnmouth, moored at the wharf, betrays the close links between this part of the Thames and the north-east coast of England. Enormous quantities of coal were shipped down from the coalfields to London as well as manufactured goods and other general supplies. Near the schooner, there are lighters, a sailing barge and watermen's skiffs. The wharf was used especially by Truman's Black Eagle brewery in Spitalfields, hence its name and the barges laden with beer barrels. Dickens, on his way to view the Wapping workhouse, loses his way and finds himself 'on a swing-bridge looking down at some dark locks in some dirty water'.

Eastern Basin, London Docks, c.1865

Many of the ships on the right of the photograph are in the process of having a refit with their fore-top masts and yards unshipped, jib-booms drawn in, and martingales, stays and rigging slackened. Dickens had a good knowledge of these docks. In the essay 'Bound for the Great Salt Lake' in *The Uncommercial Traveller* he describes a visit to them and the surrounding area of Wapping and Shadwell. Dickens boarded the *Amazon,* an emigrant ship with 800 Mormons on board, possibly moored in this dock or in the adjoining Shadwell Basin. He was curious to see 'the Latter-day saints' before they set off on their voyage to the 'Great Salt Lake' via New York.

Workers on the 'Silent Highway', 1877

Adolphe Smith, writing about men employed on barges and lighters, noted that many were 'honest, hard-working' but at the same time 'rough' and 'poorly educated'. As they were constantly on the move, it was difficult for them to 'secure education for their children' and they themselves were largely illiterate.

VIEW OF THE THAMES AND LONDON BRIDGE FROM THE CUSTOM HOUSE QUAY, c.1865

Five watermen in their skiffs pose in the foreground of the photograph. Such craft moored in front of Billingsgate Fish Market were described by Dickens as 'oyster boats and Dutchmen'. Pip in *Great Expectations* explored this part of the river where he found 'plenty of scullers going here and there . . . plenty of barges dropping down with the tide'. This was in the 1830s when 'the navigation of the river between bridges, in an open boat, was a much easier and commoner matter'. Thirty years later steamboats were much more prevalent and made life very difficult for the watermen.

Overleaf: THE POOL OF LONDON WITH THE TOWER AND WHARVES IN THE DISTANCE, c.1875

Brewer's, Chester and Galley Quays, to the left of the Tower of London, form part of the old Legal Quays, the heart of the Port of London before the enclosed docks were built at the beginning of the nineteenth century. The large warehouses in the distance, beyond the Tower, form part of the St Katharine Dock which opened in 1828. Hay barges were a distinctive feature of the river in the Victorian period. As seen here, their loads could easily be stacked three to four metres high. Enormous quantities of hay were needed for the thousands of horses at work on London's streets, pulling carts and wagons, hansom cabs and omnibuses.

Great Expectations

⌘

'At that time, the steam-traffic on the Thames was far below its present extent, and watermen's boats were far more numerous. Of barges, sailing colliers, and coasting-traders, there were perhaps, as many as now; but of steam-ships, great and small, not a tithe or a twentieth part so many. Early as it was, there were plenty of scullers going here and there that morning, and plenty of barges dropping down with the tide; the navigation of the river between bridges, in an open boat, was a much easier and commoner matter in those days than it is in these; and we went ahead among many skiffs and wherries briskly.

Old London Bridge was soon passed, and old Billingsgate Market with its oyster-boats and Dutch-men, and the White Tower and Traitor's Gate, and we were in among the tiers of shipping. Here were the Leith, Aberdeen, and Glasgow steamers, loading and unloading goods, and looking immensely high out of the water as we passed alongside; here, were colliers by the score and score, with the coal-whippers plunging off stages on deck, as counterweights to measures of coal swinging up, which were then rattled over the side into barges; here, at her moorings was to-morrow's steamer for Rotterdam, of which we took good notice; and here to-morrow's for Hamburg, under whose bowsprit we crossed. And now I, sitting in the stern, could see, with a faster beating heart, Mill Pond Bank and Mill Pond stairs.'

STEAMBOAT ON THE THAMES, BLACKWALL REACH, C.1865

This view was taken probably from the roof of the Brunswick Hotel and Tavern. Brunswick pier, just seen at bottom right of the picture, was a popular destination for locals, and Londoners in general. Many came on the railway from Fenchurch Street Station to admire the fine prospect of the river and the passing ships as well as to promenade up and down the pier. When researching the dramatic final river scenes of *Great Expectations*, Dickens hired a steamer for the day from Blackwall to Southend. This photograph reminds one of the Hamburg steamer in the book with its speed evident from the funnel's smoke and the paddlewheels' wash.

VIEW OF THE POOL OF LONDON, C.1865

This stereoscopic photograph, framed by one of the arches of London Bridge and taken from an interesting perspective on an appropriately named barge *Thames*, shows passengers boarding a steamboat at London Bridge Wharf beyond. Dickens in his essay 'The River' in *Sketches by Boz* captures the hustle and bustle of boarding a pleasure steamer there, 'A Margate boat lies alongside the wharf, the Gravesend boat (which starts first) lies alongside that again; and as a temporary communication is formed between the two, by means of a plank and hand-rail, the natural confusion of the scene is by no means diminished ... Then the bell, which is the signal for the Gravesend boat starting, begins to ring most furiously: and people keep time to the bell, by running in and out of our boat at a double-quick pace.'

INDUSTRY

Victorian London was Britain's largest manufacturing centre. At the start of the nineteenth century, the capital employed more steam engines in its enormous breweries, distilleries and vinegar works than any other part of the world. Although London was not known for its large cotton mills or iron foundries, its new factories produced innovative goods such as steam engines at Maudslay's works in Lambeth, 'improved' water closets at Bramah's in Pimlico, and continuous paper-making machines at Donkin's in Bermondsey. London supported more trades than any other city and 'London-made' stood for the highest quality. The signs of innovation were everywhere. Large gas works produced coal gas for street and shop lighting. Cast iron was used in bridge and warehouse construction, steam and hydraulic power in the docks. Brunel used a patented iron shield when building his Thames Tunnel, the world's first crossing under a navigable river and a wonder of the age when it opened in 1843.

With all the construction work going on, it is not surprising that the building trade was one of Victorian London's largest industries. Materials arrived from all over the country and were transported to builder's wharves and yards by canal, river, railway or horse-drawn cart. In the 1830s and 1840s Thomas Cubitt's depot and works at Thames Bank, Pimlico, was an extensive operation employing over 1,000 workmen. It had steam-powered sawmills and a brickworks as well as a row of workshops where smiths, masons, plumbers, glaziers, painters, carpenters and joiners made every sort of fitting and fixture needed to construct a house. The manufacture of paints, another important London trade, supported a number of related industries such as white-lead, oil and varnish, and turpentine works. By the 1870s, most of these often obnoxious trades were located in east London, on the Isle of Dogs, at Stratford and at Bow, away from fashionable residential districts.

During the nineteenth century London retained its supremacy as a producer of high-quality goods for the luxury market both at home and abroad. Workers in the 'finishing trades' such as jewellery, watchmaking and silver mounting were regarded as a 'labour artistocracy', serving a long apprenticeship and developing highly-specialised skills. These trades were concentrated in specific areas of London. For example, jewellers and watchmakers were located in the Clerkenwell area, just to the north of the City of London. Most craftsmen worked in small workshops surrounded by local suppliers of materials and hand tools. Proximity to the centre of London and small-scale production methods enabled the luxury trades to respond quickly to changes in fashion and also ensured that London retained a diverse manufacturing industry.

Towards the end of Dickens's life, in the 1860s, some industries declined and relocated outside of the metropolis, closer to raw materials and cheap labour. The sewing machine revolutionised London's clothing industry. Small, portable and readily acquired on a hire purchase or rental system, a sewing machine could be used in the home or in small workshops and did not require large factory premises. The machine accelerated the manufacturing process and enabled the mass production of cheap, affordable clothing. London's unskilled casual workforce often found employment in the 'sweated industries' producing 'slop' footwear and clothing for the cheap mass market. Primarily associated with the East End, sweated labour was characterised by the subdivision of work among a team of workers, often women, who gained experience in only one area of the manufacturing process. This labour system enabled London's ready-to-wear clothing industry to survive against competition from provincial factories. The industry thrived, however, at the expense of its workforce which endured appalling working conditions, poor pay and long hours.

Previous page, and above: **COMBE & COMPANY BREWERY, CASTLE STREET, C.1875**

The fourth largest brewery in London, Combe and Company occupied a large site to the north of Long Acre. The view down Longley Street towards Castle Street on the previous page shows the brewery buildings on either side, linked by an overhead walkway. Four burly draymen with their leather aprons stand in front of one of the brewery's drays. In the image above, the scale of the brewery's brick walls dwarfs the two men wearing top-hats and white aprons standing by the cart entrance openings. The slatted roof allowed for the steam produced in the brewing process to dissipate. In 1898, the company merged with two other London brewers to form Watney, Combe, Reid & Co. Ltd., the country's largest brewery.

OLD COURT, UPPER FORE STREET, LAMBETH, C.1865

The barrels being lowered from Alfred Hunt's chemical works probably contained phosphate of lime. Lambeth was one of London's main industrial districts and bone sorting and crushing was one of the more unpleasant and smelly trades. Animal bones were brought here from all over the capital. They were sorted first, with the better-quality ones being sold on to those who made items such as combs and handles. The rest of the bones were boiled up to extract any remaining gelatine which was used to make soap. Finally, the bones were crushed into a fine dust to be used as a fertiliser.

CHUBB, ROUND & CO.'S WORKS, WEST FERRY ROAD, MILLWALL, 1885

This remarkable photograph shows vast mounds of coconut husks waiting to be made into rope and matting. Waste at the end of the manufacturing process at this works was sold to gardeners as a soil improver. A row of terraced houses overlooks the site showing how industrial premises in London were often hemmed in on all sides. Many workers lived in close proximity to their place of employment.

MESSRS JAMES ASH & CO., CUBITT TOWN, 1863

James Ash established his own shipbuilding yard in 1862. A skilled naval architect, he had worked previously for C J Mare and the Thames Ironworks. Unfortunately, his yard closed after only four years of operation, largely as a result of the 1866 banking crash.

THE HEAVY TURNERY AND SMITH SHOP AT JOHN PENN'S FACTORY, 1863

John Penn & Sons had two large works, one a riverside site at Deptford that specialised in the manufacture of ship's boilers and the other at Blackheath Road, Greenwich, that made marine engines. The owner is probably the figure standing centre right with his hands in his pockets. He employed around 1200 men at Deptford and a further 600 workers at Greenwich.

THE SCRAP FORGE AT MESSRS PENN & SONS WORKS, 1863

'There are few engineering firms, if any, who have a more widely spread reputation than Messrs John Penn and Son. In ironclads, in frigates, in large ocean and smaller river steamers, the engines constructed by them are at work in all parts of the world, and the excellence of their design and beauty of their finish have done much to establish the character for the highest class of engineering workmanship which this country possesses . . . The forge . . . is one of the best shops of the kind we have seen . . . heavy shafts and similar articles being forged in another building open at the sides, containing the heavy steam-hammer and the necessary furnaces for working up the scrap.' (*Engineering, 1867*)

MESSRS GEORGE RENNIE AND SONS WORKS, DEPTFORD, 1863

These photographs, used to illustrate Patrick Barry's book *Dockyard Economy and Naval Power*, were taken at the highpoint of the London's shipbuilding industry. In the late 1850s, during and following the Crimean War, there was a great demand for all types of naval and supply vessels. London shipyards built many ships for the Admiralty as well as for foreign navies. At Penn & Sons' and Rennie's works, ship engines and boilers were made in large numbers. The images capture the working life of the yards and manufactories with their vast array of machinery and equipment. An overhead travelling crane at Rennie's facilitated the movement of machine and engine parts.

RICHARD TANGYE ALONGSIDE THE *GREAT EASTERN*, JANUARY 1858

The *Great Eastern*, designed by Isambard Kingdom Brunel, was built at John Scott Russell's shipbuilding yard at Millwall on the Isle of Dogs. The size of the ship required it to be constructed sideways on to the Thames. It was a great tourist attraction and on 1 June 1857 Dickens travelled by steamboat with some friends to take a look at it. Launch attempts failed, much to Brunel's embarrassment, incurring considerable financial loss. Finally, special patented hydraulic jacks, supplied by Richard Tangye, successfully shunted the *Great Eastern* into the river. Here the diminutive Richard Tangye (his height was under five feet) proudly and confidently rests his hand on one of his hydraulic jacks.

Bevington & Sons, Neckinger Mills, Bermondsey

These photographs are some of the earliest recording a London industry. They were taken by Geoffrey Bevington, one of the owners of Bevington and Sons, leather merchants and tanners of Bermondsey. The images show some of the different finishing processes and were displayed on the firm's stand at the 1862 International Exhibition. Bermondsey was the traditional home of leather processing in the capital, known for its foul-smelling pits where animal skins underwent

tanning. Bevingtons' works were one of the largest occupying the site of a former papermaking mill. The firm specialised particularly in dyed morocco leather from goat skins, used for covering coach-linings and chair covers, and for the finest bookbinding. The poster 'Layard for Southwark' records the successful parliamentary election campaign of Austen Henry Layard, the celebrated archaeologist of Assyrian sites at Nineveh and Nimrud and a good friend of Dickens.

Left: CLEANSING AND
PARING SHEEP SKINS FOR
WOOL RUGS, C.1861

Right: SPLITTING SHEEP
SKINS IN THE LIMED
CONDITION FOR SKIVER
AND CHAMOIS LEATHER,
C.1861

Below: FINISHING SKIVERS
AND PERSIANS FOR HAT
LININGS AND BOOT
PURPOSES, C.1861

The Nave from the Eastern Dome

The 1862 International Exhibition

An international exhibition was held at South Kensington in 1862, that hoped to repeat the success and profitability of the 1851 Great Exhibition. The building was constructed as a permanent structure, unlike the Crystal Palace. The Thames Iron Company supplied the wrought iron for the roof and large domes. The building was not favorably received and demolished at the end of the exhibition. The displays attracted over six million visitors. Many London manufacturers exhibited their products, including marine engines made by Rennie and Penn.

EASTERN TRANSEPT

THE NAVE FROM THE WESTERN DOME

RAILWAYS AND CONSTRUCTION

Proposals for the first railway in the metropolis were issued in 1832. However, it was not until 14 December 1836 that the first passengers were carried along the raised railroad that crossed over Bermondsey, an industrial and working class area and then on over marshland and market gardens to Deptford and Greenwich. This was a very small local undertaking compared to the London and Birmingham railway which opened in 1837, one of the most ambitious civil engineering projects up to this time. To mark the first line to connect the capital city with the Midlands and the North, the railway company built an enormous Doric entrance gate at Euston (demolished in 1961-2) which came to symbolise the arrival of the railway age in London.

Railway construction between London and regional towns and cities progressed at a very rapid pace in the 1840s. Numerous termini were constructed in the metropolis including the Great Western at Paddington, the Eastern Counties at Shoreditch (later known as Bishopsgate), the London and Southampton at Nine Elms and the London and Blackwall at Fenchurch Street. In 1846, a parliamentary committee was set up to examine the building of yet further lines in London, especially in the City. It decided that no new surface railways should be permitted within the central area south of the New Road (now known as the Marylebone and Euston Road) and west of the City Road, Finsbury Square and Bishopsgate. The lack of any one central terminus which could be used by all the different railway companies resulted in a proliferation of stations on the periphery of the built-up areas.

The railways transformed the urban and suburban landscape of London. Towering high above existing buildings, railway bridges and viaducts were seen as both an architectural and engineering triumph. The reality of life beneath the arches was, however, somewhat different. Areas in the vicinity of the railway soon became associated with urban squalor and dereliction. In 1846, a resident of East London commented 'a viaduct would not be tolerated in a respectable neighbourhood and undoubtedly renders a bad one worse'.

Initiated by industrialists and businessmen, each railway line was financed by a joint stock company with private shareholders. Railway investment became a national preoccupation as investors both small and large rushed to buy shares. The mood was captured by a cartoon in *Punch* magazine in which Queen Victoria asked her husband the 'Momentous Question', 'Tell me, oh tell me, dearest Albert, have you any Railway Shares?' Railway share mania reached a peak between 1844 and 1847 when Parliament authorised railway schemes to the value of £250 million involving 9,500 miles of line. By the end of the decade the railway bubble had burst, bringing financial ruin to many investors.

Plans suggested by Charles Pearson, the City of London Solicitor, to relieve traffic congestion by creating the world's first underground railway seemed inconceivable when first proposed. But in 1863, the Metropolitan Railway opened between Farringdon and Paddington. It was built using the 'cut and cover' method, whereby a trench was dug from the surface and lined with brick before the tracks were laid and the trench roofed over. Any buildings in the path of the trench had to be demolished, so wherever possible the railway ran beneath a road.

Despite the smells and the smoke, the railway was an instant success, and in its first year carried almost ten million passengers. The second line to be built, the Metropolitan District Railway, extended the first from Paddington to Blackfriars via Kensington, Victoria and Westminster. This was also built using the 'cut and cover' method and was begun in 1866. The last section, from Westminster to Blackfriars, was built concurrently with the Victoria Embankment and completed in 1871.

LEINSTER GARDENS, BAYSWATER, C.1867

Numbers 23 and 24 Leinster Gardens lay in the
direct path of the Metropolitan District Railway.
As it was a 'cut and cover' railway line, these houses
had to be demolished. The gap in the terrace was
later closed by a false facade with painted-on doors
and windows to match the rest of terrace. Excavated
soil has been loaded into a railway wagon.

Previous page: **VIEW OF THE METROPOLITAN
DISTRICT RAILWAY WORKS NEAR SOUTH
KENSINGTON STATION, C.1868**

It seems that a small house is in danger of falling
down as a railway cutting is being excavated. A
section of track has already been laid to enable spoil
to be removed rapidly from the site.

Dombey and Son

'THE FIRST SHOCK of a great earthquake had, just at that period, rent the whole neighbourhood to its centre. Traces of its course were visible on every side. Houses were knocked down; streets broken through and stopped; deep pits and trenches dug in the ground; enormous heaps of earth and clay thrown up; buildings that were undermined and shaking, propped by great beams of wood. Here, a chaos of carts, overthrown and jumbled together, lay topsy-turvy at the bottom of a steep unnatural hill; there, confused treasures of iron soaked and rusted in something that had accidentally become a pond. Everywhere were bridges that led nowhere; thoroughfares that were wholly impassable; Babel towers of chimneys, wanting half their height; temporary wooden houses and enclosures, in the most unlikely situations; carcases of ragged tenements, and fragments of unfinished walls and arches, and piles of scaffolding, and wildernesses of bricks, and giant forms of cranes, and tripods straddling above nothing. There were a hundred thousand shapes and substances of incompleteness, wildly mingled out of their places, upside down, burrowing in the earth, aspiring in the air, mouldering in the water, and unintelligible as any dream. Hot springs and fiery eruptions, the usual attendants upon earthquakes, lent their contributions of confusion to the scene. Boiling water hissed and heaved within dilapidated walls; whence, also, the glare and roar of flames came issuing forth; and mounds of ashes blocked up rights of way, and wholly changed the law and custom of the neighbourhood.

In short, the yet unfinished and unopened Railroad was in progress; and, from the very core of all this dire disorder, trailed smoothly away, upon its mighty course of civilisation and improvement.'

CONSTRUCTION WORK ON THE METROPOLITAN DISTRICT RAILWAY AT PRAED STREET C.1866

These two photographs, looking east and west up Praed Street, Paddington, capture the upheaval and debris caused by the building of a railway line in the centre of the built-up metropolis. In the image on the right, three women and three children stand on the first floor back roof of a tavern with the works below. Little remains of an adjoining house in the course of demolition with one chimney pot precariously perched at the top of a wall. In the other view, a group of navvies are taking a break. Their spades and pickaxes have been laid down and the base of a steam crane is used as a temporary seat for three of them. A horse and cart can be glimpsed in front of the public house with Praed Street beyond to the right.

CONSTRUCTION WORK ON THE METROPOLITAN DISTRICT RAILWAY AT PRAED STREET C.1867

The works are slightly more advanced than the previous images with the roof of the new Paddington (Praed Street) Underground station visible in the distance. The first Underground station at Paddington which opened in 1863 was to the north of the mainline terminus whereas this new line was to the south. A group of 'navvies' pose here for the camera beside a steam crane. The roof over the cutting is nearly complete. The two towers of the Great Western Railway's hotel in Praed Street can be seen behind the steam crane.

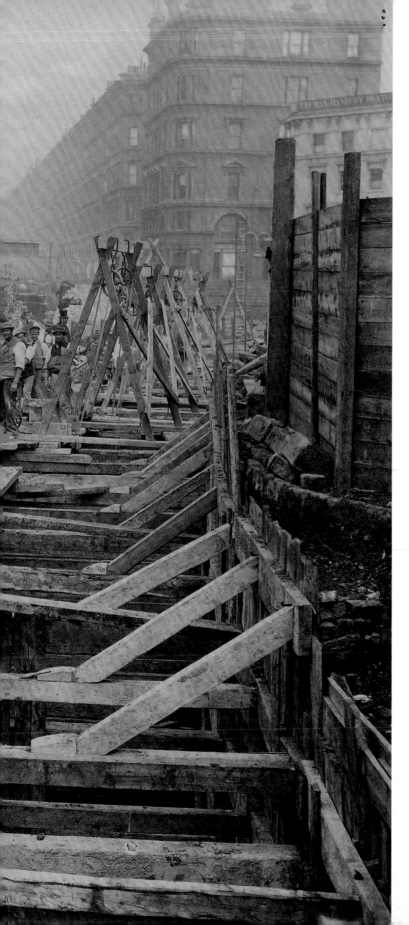

Construction work on the Metropolitan District Railway at Victoria, c.1868

The Underground line is being excavated near Victoria Street. The photograph looks west with the Windsor Castle Tavern at the junction of Vauxhall Bridge Road to the right. Victoria Station entrance is out of the picture to the right. The Victoria sewer had to be deviated from the north to the south side of the railway which involved extra work along this stretch of the line. There were further complications at Victoria Station as it was a low point, below the natural drainage level and required a pumping engine. When the Victoria Underground station was built, its walls were lined with nearly a metre of concrete in order to make it as watertight as possible.

CONSTRUCTION WORK ON THE SITE OF BLACKFRIARS STATION, C.1868

The clearance work for laying out Queen Victoria Street, a new thoroughfare in the City of London, is proceeding while the Underground railway is under construction at Blackfriars. To the lower right of the dome of St Paul's Cathedral, the church of St Andrew-by-the-Wardrobe stands alongside the substantial new offices of the British and Foreign Bible Society. Where the Metropolitan District line met the viaduct of the London Chatham and Dover Railway at Blackfriars, major works took place with very careful tunnelling, demolition of arches and the use of massive iron girders while the line above remained operational.

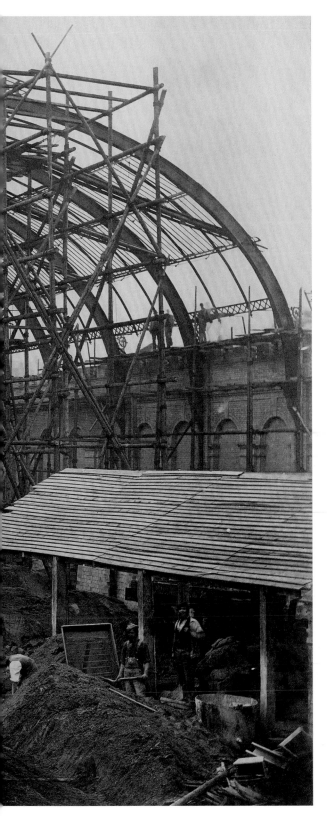

GLOUCESTER ROAD STATION
UNDER CONSTRUCTION, C.1867

This photograph shows the building method of the roofs involving a complex grid of timber scaffolding that was used to erect the iron arched ribs. Each section was assembled on site.

KENSINGTON STATION
UNDER CONSTRUCTION, C.1867

Along the line of the Metropolitan District, the roofs of the new station buildings gradually took shape. Although not on the scale of the mainline stations, the arched roofs added a new distinctive feature to London's cityscape.

PADDINGTON (PRAED STREET) STATION, 1868

Several railway workers and officials have been positioned for the camera in this view of the interior of the new Underground station at Praed Street, Paddington. The photographer's portable darkroom stands on the track.

THE TRACK AND PLATFORMS OF NOTTING HILL STATION, 1868

At the time of opening, the northern part of the station roof over the platform was intersected by Uxbridge Street. Some felt that this marred the appearance of Notting Hill Station. The view south down the tracks here shows the massive retaining walls, bridges and open aspect of this part of the Underground.

Dombey and Son

'HERE WERE RAILWAY PATTERNS in its drapers' shops, and railway journals in the windows of its newsmen. There were railway hotels, office-houses, lodging-houses, boarding-houses; railway plans, maps, views, wrappers, bottles, sandwich-boxes, and time-tables; railway hackney-coach and stands; railway omnibuses, railway streets and buildings, railway hangers-on and parasites, and flatterers out of all calculation. There was even railway time observed in clocks, as if the sun itself had given in.'

PADDINGTON (PRAED STREET) STATION, 1868.

The Underground stations were described as 'neat, substantial and well-finished buildings, well lighted and ventilated.' The elliptical iron roofs made good use of glass with zinc often filling the intermediate sections.

Gloucester Road Station, 1868

The stations of the new Metropolitan District Railway Line were designed by Sir John Fowler, the railway's engineer, and his assistants. Their Italianate style blended well with the respectable private housing estates of west London. Gloucester Road Station was larger than other station buildings with its central upper storey and two wings. Sir John Fowler was believed to be the best paid engineer in the world in the 1860s. He received a fee of £152,000 for the first Underground line between Paddington and Farrington Street and a further £157,000 for the Metropolitan District.

BAYSWATER STATION, 1868

It would seem that all the uniformed staff of the station, as well as one of the local policemen and a group of small boys, have gathered for this photo taken in front of the new Underground station.

There is still some work remaining to be completed with the wheelbarrow and pile of paving stones. Bayswater was a respectable middle-class housing district at this period.

LONDON BRIDGE STATION, c.1860

This was one of the busiest and most confusing of mid-Victorian mainline stations. The following railway companies operated services from London Bridge – the London & Brighton and South Coast Railway, the South East Railway, the London & Croydon Railway and the London and Greenwich Railway. The long line of cabs outside the entrance is indicative of the large number of passengers that arrived and departed from the station.

CANNON STREET STATION HOTEL, 1878

At many of London's mainline stations, enormous grand hotels were built, usually run by the railway companies. Cannon Street Station was designed by E M Barry and opened in 1867. The South Eastern Railway ran train services to the continent from this station and the hotel provided a convenient place to stay for merchants and businessmen visiting London. The advertising hoarding fronting Cannon Street is promoting excursions to the Paris Universal Exhibition.

AT HOME
AND IN THE STUDIO

There are relatively few surviving photographs of ordinary Londoners at home dating from the mid-nineteenth century. For their portraits, Victorians would visit photographic studios and pose against stylised and formal backgrounds, perhaps standing alongside a piece of furniture. These photographs often give insight into costume and hair styles but do not reflect the relaxed and informal postures adopted by ordinary people when at the home.

Well-known Londoners had their portraits taken and then these images were produced, marketed and sold by the photographic studios as *cartes de visite* in their thousands. It became popular to collect such photographs, adding them to albums and storing them alongside photographs of one's own family. Such photographs brought the public closer to the actual appearance of famous people. This made, for example, the face of Dickens known throughout the world and contributed to his celebrity status.

Some photographers worked outside with portable darkrooms and they tended to be found at parks and other public attractions. As interior photography was problematic, the images of domestic life were usually taken outside, in private gardens or in front of the entrance of the house. Many record family groups or a meeting of friends. These were sometimes taken by a local professional photographer. However, photography was becoming a popular amateur pastime and more often a family member would be on hand with his camera and nearby darkroom to capture the scene. A number of photographs exist of Dickens in his garden at Gad's Hill in the mid 1860s but none survive or were taken of him at any of the London houses in which he lived.

Dickens was a master at portraying the salient features of characters in his novels and stories in just a few sentences. His descriptions can seem almost as real and lifelike as a photographic portrait. A good example is his portrayal of the evil Quilp in *The Old Curiosity Shop*:

> '. . . an elderly man of remarkably hard features and forbidding aspect, and so low in stature as to be quite a dwarf, though his head and face were large enough for the body of a giant . . . But what added most to the grotesque expression of his face was a ghastly smile, which, appearing to be the mere result of habit and to have no connection with any mirthful or complacent feeling, constantly revealed the few discoloured fangs that were yet scattered in his mouth, and gave him the aspect of a panting dog.'

The initial introduction of a character fixes them in the reader's mind. A few mannerisms are identified and oddities revealed, seemingly sealing the person as a living entity. Here, for instance, is the memorable entrance of the Rev Mr Chadband in *Bleak House*

> 'Mr. Chadband is a large yellow man with a fat smile and a general appearance of having a good deal of train oil in his system . . . moves softly and cumbrously, not unlike a bear who has been taught to walk upright. He is very much embarrassed about the arms, as if they were inconvenient to him and he wanted to grovel, is very much in perspiration about the head, and never speaks without first putting up his great hand, as delivering a token to his hearers that he is going to edify them.'

Such portrait descriptions were accompanied by an engraved illustration that picked out the distinctive features of the person. Dickens is able also to include a character's movement, something which can only be suggested in a photographic portrait whether taken in a studio or at home.

Douglas William Jerrold (1803-1857)

The three striking images seen here show some of Dickens's closest friends and strongest influences. Mark Lemon met Dickens in 1843 but in 1858 their friendship foundered during the time of Dickens's separation from his wife. They were reconciled at Clarkson Stanfield's funeral in 1867. Lemon became editor of *Punch* in 1841, a post which he held until his death. They collaborated in writing the farce

Previous page: MARK LEMON (1809-1870)

Mr Nightingale's Diary (1851) and Lemon was an enthusiastic participant in Dickens's amateur theatricals. Dickens's children called him 'Uncle Porpoise'.

Douglas Jerrold's striking photograph captures the intensity of his outspoken radical views. He came from a theatrical and naval background and when he met Dickens in 1836 had already achieved spectacular stage success with *Black-Ey'd Susan* (1829). His influence was particularly

THOMAS CARLYLE (1795-1881)

evident in Dickens's most radical Christmas story, *The Chimes* (1844). Dickens was deeply shocked at Jerrold's sudden death in 1857 and threw himself into arranging benefit activities to help support his family.

Dickens wrote that he 'would go farther to see Carlyle than any man alive'. Thomas Carlyle's role as essayist, historian, and analyst of 'the condition-of-England question' made him a provocative conscience for the age and a massive influence on Dickens from their first meeting in 1840. Carlyle described Dickens as 'one of a thousand' and wrote of his 'rare and great worth as a brother man; a most cordial, sincere, clear-sighted, quietly decisive, just and loving man'. Dickens dedicated *Hard Times* to Carlyle in 1854 and drew substantially on his *History of the French Revolution* when writing *A Tale of Two Cities*. Carlyle, in his turn, attended several of Dickens's public readings, laughing uproariously all through.

Edward Bulwer-Lytton (1803–1873)

William Makepeace Thackeray (1813–1863)

Henry Wadsworth Longfellow (1807–1882)

Benjamin Disraeli (1804–1881)

Nicholas Nickleby

————— ᴄᴡ꒰ —————

'There are only two styles of portrait painting; the
serious and the smirk.'

WILLIAM WILKIE COLLINS (1824-1889)

FELLOW WRITERS

Dickens's circle of literary acquaintances and friends
was extensive. He met Wilkie Collins in 1851 and they
went on to form a close friendship and productive
literary collaboration. Collins published *The Woman
in White*, *No Name* and *The Moonstone* as serials in *All
the Year Round* as well as a large number of individual
essays and stories for that and its predecessor
Household Words. He also took part in amateur
theatricals organised by Dickens and wrote *The
Frozen Deep* (1857), through performances of which
Dickens met Ellen Ternan. Dickens and Thackeray
knew each other from 1836 when Thackeray applied
to become illustrator for *The Pickwick Papers*. The
two writers were often compared and Thackeray
described them as being both 'at the top of the tree'.
He admired Dickens's creativity and imagination
and reviewed his work enthusiastically, whilst always
being conscious of their class differences. Their
friendship went through a very difficult period
from 1858 but they were reconciled shortly before
Thackeray's death. Dickens met Longfellow during
his first American visit in 1842 and the two became
fast friends. Longfellow visited London later in 1842
and stayed with Dickens, accompanying him on a
tour of the slums. He visited Dickens again in 1856
and 1868. A highly popular and influential man of
letters, Bulwer-Lytton probably met Dickens in the
1830s. In 1850 they collaborated on the founding
of the Guild of Literature and Art and became
close friends. Dickens respected Bulwer-Lytton's
literary judgement and changed the ending of *Great
Expectations* in response to his advice. Benjamin
Disraeli was a statesman and novelist writing on
similar social themes to Dickens but their political
outlooks were significantly different.

ROBERT KEELEY (1793-1869)

MARY KEELEY (1806-1899)

CHARLES JAMES MATTHEWS (1803-1878)

JAMES SHERIDAN KNOWLES (1784-1862)

WILLIAM CHARLES MACREADY (1793-1873)

THE THEATRICAL PROFESSION

Dickens's fascination with the theatre is evident in both his life and his writings. One of his greatest friends and most long-lasting friendships was with the actor W C Macready who described him as 'a friend who really loves me'. The two men acted as godparents for one another's children. Macready's stage career began at the age of sixteen and he went on to perform at the forefront of his profession until his retirement in 1851. As well as acting, he managed Covent Garden Theatre (1837-9) and took a leading part in reviving Shakespeare's plays including a return to the original text of *King Lear* in 1838. Robert Keeley was a leading comic actor of his time, playing at all of the main London houses between 1819 and 1842. He and his wife Mary managed the Lyceum from 1844 to 1847 where they produced many adaptations from Dickens's works. Keeley played Sarah Gamp from *Martin Chuzzlewit*, for which role he was advised by Dickens. Charles James

Matthews was the son of Charles Matthews, the great comic actor much admired by Dickens, and was the outstanding light comedian performing during Dickens's lifetime. He married Madam Vestris and they co-managed Covent Garden Theatre (1839-42) and the Lyceum (1847-55). James Sheridan Knowles was a cousin of the playwright Richard Brinsley Sheridan. Dickens helped Knowles when he went bankrupt by organising benefit performances and taking part in them. Knowles became the first curator of Shakespeare's house in Stratford-upon-Avon.

TOM TAYLOR (1817-1880)   JENNIE LEE (1845-1930)

KATE TERRY (1844-1924)

Toole — Artful Dodger

JOHN LAWRENCE TOOLE (1832-1906)

IN AND OUT OF COSTUME

Tom Taylor was a dramatist, critic and biographer who also edited *Punch*. He was a prolific playwright, producing about a hundred plays, many adapted from other sources like Dickens's novels. His 1863 success *The Ticket-of-Leave Man*, presented at the Olympic Theatre in Wych Street, was the earliest example of a long-running play, with 407 consecutive performances. Kate Terry was a member of a famous theatrical family which included her sister Ellen and later her grandson, John Gielgud. Dickens wrote of her performance in his friend Edward Bulwer Lytton's play *The Lady of Lyons* (1838) in 1863, 'That is the very best piece of womanly tenderness I have ever seen on the stage, and you'll find that no audience can miss it.' She may be seen here both in stage costume and ordinary dress. A number of performers made reputations by interpreting Dickens's characters in the numerous adaptations of his works. 'Johnny' Toole, seen here in costume as the Artful Dodger was a clerk in the City of London in the early 1850s before pursuing a stage career. Dickens went to see him perform at the Walworth Literary Institution in April 1852, 'I remember what I once myself wanted in that way, and I should like to serve him'. He later

recommended Toole to Benjamin Webster at the Adelphi, noting his 'power of passion, very unusual indeed in a comic actor'. Toole had considerable success in performing Dickens characters, especially Bob Cratchit and Caleb Plummer. His interpretation of the Artful Dodger was popular on both sides of the Atlantic. He became a Vice President of The Dickens Fellowship. First appearing on the stage at the Lyceum Theatre on 22 January 1870, Jennie Lee's connection with Dickens rests with her successful interpretation of the character of Jo in *Bleak House*, which she first performed in San Francisco in an adaptation of the novel by J P Burnett. On returning to Britain, at the Globe Theatre on 22 February 1876, she opened as Jo, playing the part with 'a realism and a pathos difficult to surpass'.

John Everett Millais (1829-1896)

Effie Millais (1828-1897)

Pauline Viardot-Garcia (1821-1910)

Charlotte Helen Sainton-Dolby
(1821-1885)

WILLIAM POWELL FRITH (1819-1909)

PAINTING AND MUSIC

William Powell Frith was encouraged by Dickens when a young artist and later painted his portrait in 1859. It was a portrait much praised by those who knew him as 'the real man'. Frith's paintings like *Derby Day* and *The Railway Station* capture very well the teeming activity and variety of life in the nineteenth century as it is captured in Dickens's writing. Millais was one of the most significant members of the Pre-Raphaelite Brotherhood. His painting of *Christ in the House of His Parents* was subjected to a highly critical review by Dickens in *Household Words* in 1850. Dickens's daughter Katey modelled for Millais's *The Black Brunswicker* in 1860 and Millais drew a portrait of Dickens on his deathbed. Like a plot in one of the author's novels, 'Effie' Chalmers caused a scandal by leaving her then husband John Ruskin, claiming the marriage was unconsummated, and marrying Millais in 1855.

Charlotte Dolby was sister of George Dolby who was the third of Dickens's reading tour managers from 1866-1870. She had written to Dickens in November 1858 suggesting her brother for that role but at that point Arthur Smith was still alive and Dickens needed no replacement. Dickens admired Charlotte Dolby's talent as a contralto singer, describing her in a letter of 15 June 1857 as 'one of the finest of living artists'. Mendelssohn wrote the contralto part in *Elijah* for her voice. Pauline Viardot-Garcia was a French mezzo-soprano, who first appeared in London at Her Majesty's Theatre as Desdemona in Rossini's *Otello* on 9 May 1839. She married Louis Viardot, Director of the Théâtre Italien, Paris, in 1841 and sang every year in London between 1848 and 1858. Dickens met her in Paris in 1855 and wrote to her of his admiration of her 'great genius'.

QUEEN VICTORIA (1819-1901)

STEREOSCOPIC C°   COPYRIGHT

CHARLES DICKENS (1812-1870)

SOVEREIGN AND SUBJECT

Whilst we tend to locate Dickens firmly within the Victorian period, he was twenty-five years old in 1837 when Victoria came to the throne and was already established as a popular and successful writer as a result of *Sketches by Boz* and *The Pickwick Papers*. 'I have fallen hopelessly in love with the Queen,' Dickens wrote on the occasion of her marriage to Prince Albert in 1840. In July 1857 Dickens and a group of amateur players performed *The Frozen Deep* for the Queen at the Gallery of Illustration in London and she recorded in her journal that Dickens's interpretation of Richard Wardour was 'beyond all praise and not to be surpassed'. Queen Victoria met Dickens once, on 9 March 1870. She found him 'very agreeable, with a pleasant voice and manner' and when he died later that year she noted that he was 'a very great loss. He had a large, loving mind and the strongest sympathy with the poorer classes'. There are relatively few images of the Queen but Dickens's photograph was widely reproduced and circulated. He commented on this phenomenon as 'a melancholy fact, but I don't see the remotest chance of my interesting countenance being ever photographed, of my own knowledge and consent, again. If I were to begin, I could never leave off.'(Dickens to William Telbin, 15 March 1858)

This set of stereoscopic ambrotype photographs (positive images on glass) taken by William Henry Stratton in around 1860 capture a typical middle-class family at home in South London. They consist of intimate images of a family and servants, sometimes captured in artistic poses in an ordinary setting. Stratton described himself as a tobacconist of 179 Lambeth Walk when he filed for a patent in 1856 for 'improvements in the fire doors of furnace'.

At this period, his family house was located at 133 Kennington Road. No doubt he was a keen amateur photographer and enjoyed using his stereoscopic camera to record the gatherings of family and friends. He would have had to develop the glass ambrotypes himself. Their home-made aspect is also conveyed by the decorative coloured papers that he used to frame the two images.

STREETS AND BRIDGES

Victorian photographs of London reveal a varied streetscape made up of old and new buildings. This is particularly evident in the elevations of houses, shops and offices fronting the capital's main thoroughfares. Each decade of the nineteenth century saw old buildings demolished with the original property plots combined to create larger and taller structures in the latest fashionable style.

Perhaps the most spectacular change in the West End was the construction of a gracious park and a grand new route right through the central part of Regency London. The scheme was the creation of the architect John Nash, a close associate of the Prince Regent, later George IV. The new street, Regent's Street, was driven north from Carlton House through a part of Soho and on up to the newly laid-out Regent's Park. The route was lined with fine buildings and the park surrounded with palace-like terraces of private houses. Town planning on such a grand scale had not been seen before in the capital. When Dickens arrived in London in the early 1820s most of this scheme would have been completed.

John Nash also 'improved' St James's Park and part of the Strand, and laid out a new open space around Charing Cross. He stated that 'to add to the beauty of the approach from Westminster to Charing-cross, a square or crescent, open to, and looking down, Parliament-street' should be created. This new public space was to become Trafalgar Square. It took some years to build and the area would have been a construction site until the early 1840s.

Old London Bridge was a bridge that Dickens knew well. It featured prominently in *Oliver Twist* as the location where Nancy meets Mr Brownlow at night with Noah Claypole overhearing their conversation. David Copperfield described his 'favourite lounging-place' as 'one of the stone recesses' of old London Bridge where he would watch 'the people going by' and 'look over the balustrades at the sun shining in the water, and lighting up the golden flame on the top of the Monument.'

The bridge had become structurally unsafe as well as inadequate for the amount of traffic using it by the start of the nineteenth century. After a competition and lengthy deliberations, the government selected the design of John Rennie, the great bridge engineer who had constructed Waterloo and Southwark Bridges. Although he died in 1821, even before his design was approved, his son John carried through his scheme and oversaw the bridge's construction. The site of the new bridge was just over thirty metres to the west of the old one. It was necessary to keep the old bridge open while the new bridge was being built alongside. This made it very difficult to construct the new bridge's foundations and piers. Gradually, the five arches of the new bridge took shape but it was dangerous work with more than forty labourers losing their lives. The new London Bridge took more than seven years to build and was opened by William IV and Queen Adelaide on August 1, 1831. It remained London's busiest bridge throughout the nineteenth century, especially after a railway station had been established close to its southern approaches.

REGENT'S STREET, C.1890

In the mid Victorian period, Regent's
Street, with its wide pavements,
had become one of London's most
fashionable shopping streets. Scott
Adie, on the left, at the corner of Vigo
Street, promoted its shop as 'Her
Majesty's Royal Tartan Warehouse'.
It specialised in tweeds, Highland
waterproof cloaks and hand-knit
Scotch hosiery.

Previous page: **VICTORIA TOWER
FROM THE SOUTH, C.1867**

The tower looms over the houses
and shops along Millbank Street.
The buildings on the right were
demolished to make way for Victoria
Tower Gardens in the early twentieth
century. The photograph was taken
very close to Church Street (now
Dean Stanley Street). This was where
Jenny Wren, the dolls' dressmaker,
in *Our Mutual Friend* lived. Dickens
wrote that in 'this region are a certain
little street called Church Street, and
a certain little blind square, called
Smith Square, in the centre of which
last retreat is a very hideous church
with four towers at the four corners,
generally resembling some petrified
monster, frightful and gigantic, on its
back with its legs in the air.'

REGENT ST., LONDON.   3383A   G.W.W.

Cheapside with Bow Church, c.1875

This photograph looking east down Cheapside shows St Mary-le-Bow Church on the right. To be a true-born Londoner or Cockney one needed to be born within the sound of Bow bells. Cheapside was a street epitomising the wealth and splendour of the commercial Victorian metropolis, with its extensive shops and businesses. It also provided a thoroughfare into the city for many, like the young Charles Dickens in 1822 and one of his fictional heroes, Pip in *Great Expectations* who came into its 'ravel of traffic' there and was 'frayed about'. The chaotic activity of Cheapside is wonderfully captured in this view with omnibuses, hansom cabs, carts, costermongers and shop windows attracting pedestrians.

Farringdon Road from the Tower of St Andrew's Holborn, looking north, c.1862

This photograph shows a new improvement scheme underway. A vast stretch of a so-called 'rookery' or slum area centred on Saffron Hill and the Fleet Valley has been swept away. Farringdon Street, a new wide thoroughfare, has been created in its place. The white single-storied building under construction in the middle foreground is Farringdon Station, the city terminus of the Metropolitan Railway, the world's first Underground line. The location of Fagin's den in *Oliver Twist* was in Field Lane close to Saffron Hill.

Kensington High Street, c.1865

Many of London's main streets were widened in the Victorian period. This view looking west shows a section of Kensington High Street opposite St Mary Abbots Church, just ten metres wide at its narrowest point. It was reported that this stretch was 'totally inadequate to the public requirements' and caused 'fatal accidents' and 'serious blockages in the traffic'. The buildings on the left fronting the street were demolished in the late 1860s. The photograph shows a gang of street cleaners at work with their brooms and their carts behind for taking away the mud and rubbish.

View of the City of London looking east, from the top of the Monument, c.1870

The densely packed and slightly disorganised perspective of the City from the Monument is punctuated with the tower of the Coal Exchange in the right foreground and in the distance the Custom House and the Tower of London. In *Martin Chuzzlewit*, the view from the rooftop of Todger's lodgings revealed 'steeples, towers, belfries, shining vanes, and masts of ships; a very forest. Gables, housetops, garret-windows, wilderness upon wilderness. Smoke and noise enough for all the world at once.'

HOLBORN, C.1860

This view looks east from a point close to the junction of Gray's Inn Road towards Holborn Hill with the tower of St Andrews, Holborn on right. On the left-hand side, the building with the impressive Doric columns is Furnival's Inn which had been rebuilt in 1818. Charles Dickens lived in chambers here between 1834 and 1837 where he wrote the first part of *The Pickwick Papers*. In his last unfinished novel, *The Mystery of Edwin Drood*, Mr Grewgious secures accommodation in a hotel there for Rosa Bud.

OLD HOUSES IN WYCH STREET, 1876

Wych Street formed an extension to the southeastern end of Drury Lane. This area remained like this until the Aldwych-Kingsway improvement scheme took place and altered this whole area: demolition began here in 1900. Wych Street had a number of theatres, including the Olympic where Tom Taylor's long-running success *The Ticket-of-Leave Man*, was performed in 1863. Dickens's friend Mark Lemon was for a time the licensee of The Shakespeare Head at 31 Wych Street. The church of St Clement Danes can be seen in the distance and Dickens set the marriage of the London landlady Mrs Lirriper there.

Old Houses in Drury Lane, 1876

Drury Lane was a busy street with a number
of business premises including a coal and coke
merchant, a watchmaker and a mission society
shown here in these two photographs from different
viewpoints. In 1890, these seventeenth-century
houses were demolished and ten years later many of
the surrounding streets were also removed as part of
the Aldwych-Kingsway improvement scheme. The
gabled property was originally a tavern, The Cock
and Magpie. The poverty of the area was borne out
by the construction of Peabody Trust buildings in

Wild Street and Drury Lane in 1882 to re-house
slum dwellers and the deserving poor. Dickens
uses Drury Lane as the setting in a number of his
novels but most powerfully in *Bleak House* with 'a
hemmed-in churchyard, pestiferous and obscene'
as the last resting place of Captain Hawdon in a
pauper's grave. The churchyard is now Drury Lane
Gardens. The church in the distance is St Mary le
Strand where Dickens's parents John and Elizabeth
(née Barrow) were married in 1809.

Shop in Macclesfield Street, Soho, 1883

Alfred Marks in *Relics of Old London* identified this shop as possible the oldest in London dating it to 1690. Parts of Macclesfield Street were demolished when Shaftesbury Avenue was constructed, opening in 1886. It is architecturally an imposing building with classical features, and its function as a general grocery shop can be seen from advertisements for Oriental Blended Teas and Ginger Beer as well as by the joint of ham and other produce in the windows. The aproned figures on the steps may well be the shop owner and the delivery boy, whilst a bearded and hatted customer looks through the shop windows.

SHOP IN BREWER STREET, SOHO, 1878

The fashionable nature of Soho in the eighteenth century is reflected by this image of a druggist shop at the junction of Lower James Street and Brewer Street, with its Doric columns conveying an air of respectable solidity and wealth. When this photograph was taken, the area had declined into a maze of passages and courts which had become a breeding ground for crime and disease with serious outbreaks of cholera in the 1850s and 1860s. The shop assistant may be seen observing the photographer with interest through the shop doorway.

STRAND, LONDON, LOOKING WEST.   417

STRAND, LONDON, LOOKING WEST, C.1890

This image shows a broad view of the Strand looking west, taken from in front of St Mary le Strand. At this period, behind the church to the east, the narrow Holywell Street ran parallel to the north of the Strand, with Wych Street nearby. These streets would be swept away as part of Aldwych-Kingsway development in the early twentieth century. On the left stands Somerset House, where Dickens's father John worked as a clerk for the Navy Pay Office. The offices of *The Morning Chronicle* where Dickens worked as a reporter were at 332 Strand, and the thoroughfare appears frequently in his novels. Dick Swiveller in *The Old Curiosity Shop* ran out of credit in many of the shops in the area leaving him with just one avenue to the Strand left open to him.

HOLBORN VIADUCT, C. 1875

Holborn Viaduct bridges the valley of the now subterranean River Fleet and was built between 1863 and 1869, costing over two million pounds to complete. There are staircases to enable access to Farringdon Street below. The photograph shows the backs of the two southern statues on the viaduct by Henry Bursill which represent Commerce and Agriculture. The City of London arms are positioned in the centre with winged lions at either end of the parapet. In a niche in the building flanking the viaduct on the right a sculpture can be seen of Sir Hugh Myddelton, an early 17th century City merchant and promoter of the New River scheme. Between 1874 and 1990 Holborn Viaduct station stood near here. In the process of its construction it swept away locations which Dickens had recorded particularly graphically in *Oliver Twist* such as the whole Field Lane area at the lower end of Saffron Hill, where he had set Fagin's den to which the Artful Dodger brings Oliver on his arrival in London.

KING WILLIAM STREET, C.1875

King William Street was constructed between 1829 and 1835. It was designed as an approach road to Rennie's new London Bridge. The hustle and bustle in the street delivering various kinds of merchandise reminds us of Victorian London's importance as a commercial centre. The advertising on the buildings includes encouragements to travel, something increasingly in vogue as the nineteenth century proceeded.

Old Houses in Bermondsey Street, 1881

Bermondsey at this period was an area of goods yards, biscuit making and leatherwork. Nearly all the tanneries of London were situated within its borders. Henry Dixon's photograph includes two leatherworkers, either shoemakers or cobblers, standing at the entrance to their establishment.

The houses themselves are described as 'good specimens of the houses of the time of Elizabeth and somewhat later; the frame of massive timber, else mere shells of lath and plaster; but though often out of shape and leaning in all directions, wonderfully durable.'

Old Houses in Borough High Street, Southwark, 1881

The busy commercial nature of Borough High Street in Southwark is evident from the range of goods on display in the shops shown here. On the left, a well-stocked shoe shop displays its wares while on the right the joints and portions of meat are set out and hang in a butcher's shop. This is a part of London Dickens knew well from his regular visits here when his family were in the Marshalsea Prison in 1824.

Previous page:

BLACKMAN STREET, BOROUGH, C.1890

Blackman Street links Borough High Street with Newington Causeway. In the centre in the distance is the Church of St George the Martyr. Beyond and behind the church was the site of the Marshalsea Prison between 1811 and 1842. Lodgings were found in Lant Street, the turning off to the left, for the twelve-year-old Charles Dickens. This allowed him to be close to his family in the debtor's prison whilst working at Warren's blacking factory. When he 'took possession of (his) new abode, (he) thought it was paradise'. St George's Church is sometimes known as 'Little Dorrit's church'. She was born in the nearby prison and baptised in the church. She spends a night sleeping on the parish registers when she returns too late to be admitted to the prison and she is married to Arthur Clennam there at the end of *Little Dorrit*. The character is depicted in the stained glass in the east window of St George's.

SHAFTESBURY HOUSE, ALDERSGATE STREET, 1879

Thanet House designed by Inigo Jones in 1644 shown here at 35-38 Aldersgate Street had by 1720 become an inn and subsequently a hospital in 1750, which function, as The City Lying-In Hospital, it continued to perform until 1771 and its removal to City Road. The building then became the first general dispensary for London until 1850 and, as can be seen here, became shops thereafter until its demolition in 1882.

Old Houses in Aldersgate Street, c.1879

These two photographs show the type of 17th century houses that survived in parts of the city until the late 19th century. The building called Shakespeare's House is described in 1828 as 'an old building, formerly the Half Moon Tavern'. Between then and its subsequent demolition in 1879 it was turned into a tenement building. This photograph captures it shortly before its demolition the same year. The area's decline can be seen in the 'To Let' notice in the window of one of the images. The area around Aldersgate Street features in Dickens last unfinished book, *The Mystery of Edwin Drood*. John Jasper stays in 'a hybrid hotel in a little square behind Aldersgate Street, near the General Post Office.' Dickens suffered from a fistula which he blamed on spending too much time seated at his writing desk. He was treated at the Fistula Infirmary in Aldersgate Street by the surgeon Frederick Salmon. Dickens celebrated the success of his novel *Nicholas Nickleby* at the Albion Hotel here in 1839.

nver house bore the sign of 'The Three Crowns' corner of Bedfor

CORNER OF BEDFORD STREET, COVENT GARDEN, C.1870

Dickens as a boy worked in Jonathan Warren's blacking factory in Chandos Street after it had moved there from Old Hungerford Stairs. He wrote,

> 'Next to the shop at the corner of Bedford Street in Chandos Street are two rather old-fashioned houses and shops adjoining one another. They were one then, or thrown into one, for the blacking-business; and had been a butter-shop. Opposite to them was, and is, a public-house, where I got my ale, under these new circumstances. The stones in the street may be smoothed by my small feet going across to it at dinner-time, and back again.'

HAYMARKET, C.1860

This photograph looks up the Haymarket on a summer's day with the Haymarket Theatre's portico extending to the edge of the pavement. In 1858, Ellen Ternan, a young actress and Dickens's new companion, was appearing in a number of plays at the theatre including Shakespeare's *Much Ado About Nothing* where she performed the role of Hero.

OLD HOUSES IN ALDGATE HIGH STREET, 1883

This photograph shows a row of houses demolished
for the extension of the Metropolitan Railway
from Aldgate to Tower Hill. It captures the city
going through a process of change, with the
butchers' shops operating as they must have done
for centuries, carcases hanging outside and meat
displayed on open counters; the brewers' dray
outside the Turk's Head at 71 Aldgate High Street (at
the south side, near the junction with the Minories)
is laden with casks. At the same time, more modern
modes of transport are implied by the City Bicycle
School and new inventions by the advertisement
for Singer's Sewing Machines. There are many
associations with Dickens in this area: in one of

The Uncommercial Traveller essays called 'On An
Amateur Beat' he writes of this area,

> 'A single stride at Houndsditch Church. . . a
> single stride, and everything is entirely changed
> in grain and character. West of the stride, a
> table, or a chest of drawers on sale, shall be of
> mahogany and French-polished; east of the
> stride, it shall be of deal, smeared with a cheap
> counterfeit resembling lip-salve. West of the
> stride, a penny loaf or bun shall be compact and
> self-contained; east of the stride, it shall be of a
> sprawling and splay-footed character, as seeking
> to make more of itself for the money.'

BLACKFRIARS BRIDGE WITH THE CITY IN THE DISTANCE.

BLACKFRIARS BRIDGE WITH THE CITY IN THE DISTANCE, C.1860 AND C.1875

The old 18th century stone Blackfriars Bridge had been repaired in the late 1830s with its balustrades removed and roadway and pedestrian walkway lowered. As a boy Dickens might have passed across this bridge on his journey to and from work between his lodgings in Lant Street near the Marshalsea Prison and his work place at Hungerford Stairs and later at Chandos Street. A completely new bridge, designed by Joseph Cubitt, with five iron arches was constructed in the 1860s. Just to the east of it, another bridge was built for the London, Chatham, and Dover Railway between 1862 and 1864. The iron lattice girder structure can be seen with a number of tall riverside warehouses beyond.

CANNON STREET RAILWAY BRIDGE, C.1875

Originally named the Alexandra Bridge after
Princess Alexandra of Denmark who was the wife of
the future King Edward VII, the bridge was opened
in 1866 after three years' construction. Designed
by John Hawkshaw and JohnWolfe-Barry, it was
designed to carry the South Eastern railway across
the Thames.

LONDON BRIDGE, c.1875

This dramatic photograph shows the bridge thronged with vehicles and pedestrians. So great was the level of traffic across London Bridge, especially in the morning and early evening, that in the 1850s proposals were made to widen the bridge. In 1902, the width of the pedestrian pavements increased by one metre.

SUBURBS

When Dickens arrived in the capital as a young boy, London's rising population and wealth was fuelling a 'march of bricks and mortar' over the surrounding countryside around the edge of the city. One-time villages such as Hackney, Islington and Kensington lost their sense of separateness as speculative housing covered over the green fields between. In 1822, William Cobbett noted the pace of development on the main route out of London towards Croydon; there were, 'erected within these four years, two entire miles of stock-jobbers' houses on this one road, and the work goes on with accelerated force'. Some house builders made fortunes, and left indelible marks on the map of London; Thomas Cubitt constructed acres of new houses in Bloomsbury, Belgravia and Pimlico as well as Clapham and Camden Town. With new houses came new roads. By the 1830s a new generation of well-off Londoners was commuting to and from its smart houses in the inner suburbs. London's first omnibus was introduced in 1829 between Paddington and the Bank.

Dickens, as a young man, would often venture out into the suburbs, sometimes on foot, on horseback and at other times in a pony and trap. He believed that periods of extreme mental exertion were best countered by physical exercise of a similar intensity. He was fond of walking the 'green lanes' outside town. He liked nothing better than day trips out of London to places such as Richmond, Neasden, Willesden and Greenwich. John Forster, his friend and biographer, noted how they rode out 'fifteen miles on the Great North Road, and after dining at the Red Lion in Barnet on our way home, distinguished the already memorable day by bringing in both hacks dead lame'. Dickens rented cottages in Twickenham and Finchley for his family to spend the summer months. These places were then rural retreats, but close enough for Dickens to make excursions back into town if necessary.

Londoners lived in an ever-expanding geographical area as the city engulfed surrounding towns, villages and countryside. Various factors drove suburban growth. Land in central London was increasingly used for non-residential purposes. More and more people were attracted to suburban living. Improved transport links made it easier to live further from work. Many migrants from rural areas joined the newly-arrived city-dwellers in the suburbs. New shops, markets, schools, social venues and churches gradually arrived to service this growing suburban population.

With the arrival of suburban railway routes in the 1860s, many of London's outlying villages and nearby towns were served by a fast and regular train service. For those with sufficient means, travelling became easier and places seemed closer at hand. Many men commuted into the City of London by train during the week and women made shopping expeditions to the West End. Dickens's companion, Ellen Ternan, lived in Slough in the late 1850s and then later in Peckham in the 1860s, both places that had good railway connections.

By the time of Dickens's death, railway lines extended even further into the centre of the metropolis. At London Bridge Station, to alleviate the pressure of passenger arrivals and departures, a short feeder line ran to Cannon Street Station (1866), serving the City, and a further line running west to the site of the Hungerford Market, took the railway right into the West End at Charing Cross (1864). The London, Chatham and Dover Railway crossed the river directly to the east of Blackfriars Bridge with a station at Ludgate Hill (1864-65), close to St Paul's Cathedral. Victoria Station became a major terminus for Westminster served by a railway bridge to the south, close to Battersea Park. To the west, new lines criss-crossed the landscape as further suburban parts were linked to the railway network for the first time.

Previous page: **COLNEY HATCH LANE, FRIERN BARNET, C.1870, WILLIAM ATTWOOD**

Colney Hatch was a sparsely populated part of Middlesex, some ten kilometres north of the centre of London. The main Victorian development sited in the area was the extensive second Middlesex County Lunatic Asylum which had opened in 1851 and accommodated over 1,000 patients.

VIEW LOOKING SOUTH-EAST OVER LANCASTER ROAD TOWARDS THE CRYSTAL PALACE, C.1870

This photograph by William Strudwick gives a rural feeling to West Dulwich in South London. On the right, Rosendale Road and Croxted Lane beyond are starting to be lined with houses. One senses that it will not be long before the open ground in the foreground will be divided up for further housing developments. In the distance, the Crystal Palace occupies a commanding position at the south-western edge of the ridge known as Sydenham Hill. One of the two water towers, visible to the left of the main building, raised water to a sufficient height to work two massive fountains in the gardens of the attraction. Visitors to the Crystal Palace could climb up the 400 steps to the top for spectacular views over London and the surrounding counties.

CRYSTAL PALACE, SYDENHAM, C.1890

CRYSTAL PALACE, SYDENHAM, C.1890

After the closure of the Great Exhibition in October 1851, a private company, founded by Joseph Paxton, bought and dismantled the building. It was moved from Hyde Park and re-erected to a slightly different and larger design in Sydenham. The new Crystal Palace opened on 10 June 1854 and rapidly became a major leisure attraction. To the south-east of the building, an extensive range of ornamental gardens were set out with terraces, fountains and landscaped grounds. Visitors could reach the site by railway.

Inside, a series of elaborate architectural courts had been created with displays of art drawn from different cultures and periods. Facing the Egyptian Court, there were palms and water features with a line of sphinxes, culminating in an enormous 30-metre-high sculpture of two seated figures copied from the temple at Abu Simbel. In the Victorian period these were thought to represent 'guardian deities' but are now known to be of the pharaoh himself, Rameses II.

INTERIOR OF THE CRYSTAL PALACE, C.1860

THE CRYSTAL PALACE AND GARDENS, C.1860

Photography on the Common, 1877 and 'Mush-Fakers' and Ginger-Beer Makers, 187

There were a number of enterprising street traders who operated in London's Victorian parks and open spaces, such as Clapham Common in South London. Some earned a living from photographing those who were passing by such as the nurses charged with looking after the babies and children of wealthy inhabitants in the area. Others hired out donkeys for a leisurely ride in the park. 'Mush-Fakers' or umbrella sellers sold their wares on sunny days but their business really needed an unexpected shower or thunderstorm to prosper. They also made money from repairing umbrellas on the spot. Mrs Gamp, one of Dickens's most famous fictional creations, carried a remarkable umbrella where 'a circular patch of lively blue has been dexterously let in at the top.' Dickens, also, noted the musky smell of damp umbrellas. Ginger beer was sold from barrows situated at the edge of the parks. The best time for the retailers was when the public houses were closed on Sunday mornings.

The Oval, c.1875

A cricketer with his bat sits in the foreground while on the other side of the pitch, beyond the players and umpires, a row of spectators are watching *the* match. Dickens described a cricket match in the *Pickwick Papers*. He observed the strange posture of the fielders, who 'each fixed himself into the proper attitude by placing one hand on each knee, and stooping very much as if he were "making a back" for some beginner at leap-frog.' The Oval had been established as a cricket ground in 1846 on the site of a market garden. Grass turf from Tooting Common was laid down to make the pitch. Football was also played here resulting in the Oval becoming probably the major sports ground in London during the second half of the nineteenth century. On the south side of the Oval, beyond the wooden fence on the right, can be seen part of the Phoenix Gas Works which had a large telescopic gas holder used for storing the gas.

Newington Butts, Kennington, c.1870

Newington Butts, once just a small village situated to the south of the Elephant and Castle, had become by the middle of the nineteenth century a busy middle-class suburb with a row of shops. This view, taken on a summer's day, looking north from the junction of Kennington Park Road and Lower Kennington Lane, depicts the church of St Mary Newington which was shortly to be demolished and replaced by a new church. Mr Vholes's father in *Bleak House* lived 'in an earthy cottage situated in a damp garden at Kennington'.

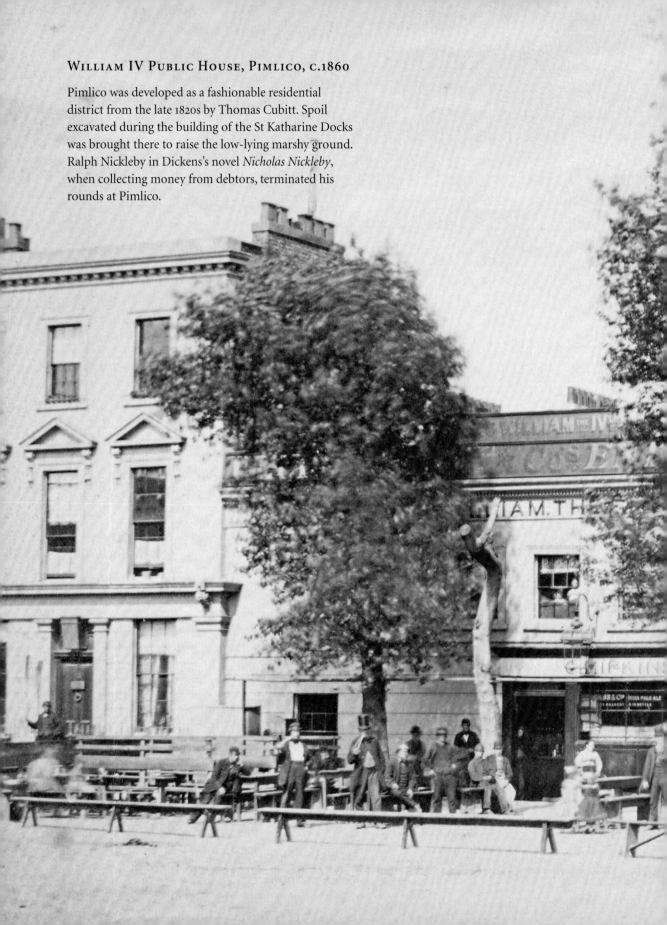

WILLIAM IV PUBLIC HOUSE, PIMLICO, c.1860

Pimlico was developed as a fashionable residential district from the late 1820s by Thomas Cubitt. Spoil excavated during the building of the St Katharine Docks was brought there to raise the low-lying marshy ground. Ralph Nickleby in Dickens's novel *Nicholas Nickleby*, when collecting money from debtors, terminated his rounds at Pimlico.

THE THAMES, HAMPTON COURT BRIDGE. 7441 J.V.

THE THAMES AND HAMPTON COURT BRIDGE, c.1885

Hampton Court and the surrounding area was a popular weekend resort of Londoners. Wherries and punts could be hired from both sides of the river. Here, in the foreground, next to the Castle Hotel, where the river Mole flows into the Thames, a barge is loaded with coal. Wealthy City merchants, bankers and civil servants owned or rented large houses in the area. Mr Gowan's mother in Dickens's *Little Dorrit* lived here. The author described such people as 'bohemians' or 'venerable inhabitants . . . encamped there like a sort of civilised gypsies' with 'a temporary air about their establishments as if they were going away the moment they could get anything better'.

VIEW AT THE FERRY, CLIVEDEN, 1866

This photograph of the Thames at Cliefden, or Cliveden, near Taplow shows the densely wooded scenery in the vicinity. This was a popular leisure destination with Victorian Londoners who travelled by train from Paddington to Maidenhead and then hired rowing skiffs, punts or even steam launches to enjoy the river between Taplow and Cookham. Nearby was the large country house, Cliveden, which had been rebuilt in the early 1850s after a fire. It was designed in the Italianate style by the architect Sir Charles Barry.

VIEW OF RICHMOND BRIDGE, 1866

As a young married man, Dickens enjoyed this part of the Thames in the summer months. He stayed at Petersham and enjoyed the 'country air' and outdoor life. With the painter Daniel Maclise and the journalist Thomas Beard, his best man and oldest friend, he played games such as quoits and bowling. He also undertook 'swimming feats from Petersham to Richmond Bridge' rising at six o'clock and plunging 'head foremost into the water to the astonishment and admiration of all beholders'.

Our Mutual Friend

'Plashwater Weir Mill Lock looked tranquil and pretty on an evening in the summer time. A soft air stirred the leaves of the fresh green trees, and passed like a smooth shadow over the river, and like a smoother shadow over the yielding grass. The voice of the falling water, like the voices of the sea and the wind, were as an outer memory to a contemplative listener; but not particularly so to Mr Riderhood, who sat on one of the blunt wooden levers of his lock-gates, dozing. Wine must be got into a butt by some agency before it can be drawn out; and the wine of sentiment never having been got into Mr Riderhood by any agency, nothing in nature tapped him.

As the Rogue sat, ever and again nodding himself off his balance, his recovery was always attended by an angry stare and growl, as if, in the absence of any one else, he had aggressive inclinations towards himself. In one of these starts the cry of "Lock, ho! Lock!" prevented his relapse into a doze. Shaking himself as he got up like the surly brute he was, he gave his growl a responsive twist at the end, and turned his face down-stream to see who hailed.

It was an amateur-sculler, well up to his work though taking it easily, in so light a boat that the Rogue remarked: "A little less on you, and you'd a'most ha' been a Wagerbut"; then went to work at his windlass handles and sluices, to let the sculler in. As the latter stood in his boat, holding on by the boat-hook to the woodwork at the lock side, waiting for the gates to open, Rogue Riderhood recognised his "T'other governor," Mr Eugene Wrayburn; who was, however, too indifferent or too much engaged to recognise him.

The creaking lock-gates opened slowly, and the light boat passed in as soon as there was room enough, and the creaking lock-gates closed upon it, and it floated low down in the dock between the two sets of gates, until the water should rise and the second gates should open and let it out. When Riderhood had run to his second windlass and turned it, and while he leaned against the lever of that gate to help it to swing open presently, he noticed, lying to rest under the green hedge by the towing-path astern of the Lock, a Bargeman.

The water rose and rose as the sluice poured in, dispersing the scum which had formed behind the lumbering gates, and sending the boat up, so that the sculler gradually rose like an apparition against the light from the bargeman's point of view. Riderhood observed that the bargeman rose too, leaning on his arm, and seemed to have his eyes fastened on the rising figure.

But, there was the toll to be taken, as the gates were now complaining and opening. The T'other governor tossed it ashore, twisted in a piece of paper, and as he did so, knew his man.

"Ay, ay? It's you, is it, honest friend?" said Eugene, seating himself preparatory to resuming his sculls. "You got the place, then?"'

MEDMENHAM FERRY, 1866

Samuel Carter Hall writing in 1859 referred to 'the adjacent country' in this area as 'exceedingly beautiful, varied by alternative mills, islands, meadows, and hills, with every now and then ornamental "forest trees" hanging over the stream, and giving pleasant shade to the current on its downward flow.'

Maple-Durham Lock and Weir, 1866

The Victorians considered the scenery along this stretch of the river Thames as exceptional. Carter Hall described it as 'an assemblage of choice picturesque objects, such as are not often met with even singly and are very rarely encountered grouped together into one picture as we here find them. At one view we have Maple-Durham ferry, lock and weir – the mossy old mill embosomed in rich foliage, from which again rises the grey church tower, behind which, though almost hidden by lofty trees, we see the turreted outline of Maple-Durham house, forming altogether a painter's paradise.'

Marsh Mills, 1866

In Dickens's *Our Mutual Friend*, Betty Higden finally reaches a mill near Henley alongside the river Thames, 'There now arose in the darkness, a great building, full of lighted windows. Smoke was issuing from a high chimney in the rear of it, and there was the sound of a water-wheel at the side. Between her and the building, lay a piece of water, in which the lighted windows were reflected, and on its nearest margin was a plantation of trees . . . She crept among the trees to the trunk of a tree whence she could see, beyond some intervening trees and branches, the lighted windows, both in their reality and their reflection in the water.'

TEDDINGTON WEIR, 1866

This stretch of river alongside Teddington Weir was often lined with anglers. They caught especially barbels, a carp-like fish, which fed on the rotting vegetation in the autumn months.

THAMES DITTON, 1866

This small village was a popular destination for London anglers. The Swan Inn was where they ate and drank overlooking the river.

WINDSOR CASTLE, 1866

This view of Windsor Castle across the Thames would have been familiar to Dickens. His son Charley attended Eton College between 1850 and 1852 and Dickens made several visits to him, taking him and his friends out for boating expeditions on this stretch of river.

Busk's Lane, Winchmore Hill and Blind Lane Brook, Osidge, c.1870.

There were many quiet leafy lanes around London. Hedges, brick walls and fences marked out the boundaries of the gardens of large houses and villas that had been built for wealthy Londoners who had moved out of the centre of the metropolis.

Dickens was very fond of walking both in the city and in the suburbs surrounding London. His friend John Forster received many letters with messages like 'What a brilliant morning for a country walk' or 'Is it possible that you can't, oughtn't, shouldn't, mustn't, *won't* be tempted, this gorgeous day?' or 'I start precisely – precisely, mind – at half-past one. Come, come, *come*, and walk in the green lanes. You will work the better for it all the week. Come! I shall expect you' or 'You don't feel disposed, do you, to muffle yourself up and start off with me for a good brisk walk over Hampstead Heath?.'

SHOPS ON THE GREEN, WINCHMORE HILL, C.1870

WINCHMORE HILL STATION, C.1871

These two photographs were taken soon after
Winchmore Hill station opened in 1871. Before the
coming of the Enfield branch of the Great Northern
Railway, Winchmore Hill was little more than an
isolated hamlet in the north London borough of
Southgate. By the First World War, Winchmore Hill
had become swamped by middle-class suburban
housing.

MANOR TOLL, GREEN LANES, 1874

In the 1860s and 1870s, Green Lanes and Seven
Sisters Road were heavily used to carry building
materials for new housing developments at Muswell
Hill and the Alexandra Palace. This resulted in the
road needing considerable repair. The toll house
keeper would have kept a watch on these works as
well as the passing wagons and carts.

View over Lancaster Road towards Norwood Cemetery, 1870

This photograph looks south over fields towards the South Metropolitan Cemetery. In the middle foreground, the Effra can be made out, marked by the trees growing along the river's winding course. This was prime suburban building land, especially as the London and Croydon Railway line ran nearby. Mr Spenlow in *David Copperfield* had a house in Norwood as did Mr Carker in *Dombey and Son*. The locality was described as a 'within easy range and reach of the great city of London' and a 'green and wooded country'. The cemetery which had opened in 1837 was one of seven new out-of-town London burial sites. It was built on a hill and the Dissenters' chapel, catacombs and Episcopal Church dominated the surrounding landscape.

LANDMARKS (NEW LONDON)

Fire was the major hazard of the nineteenth century for landmark structures and took its toll on many of them. Leading theatres such as Drury Lane and Covent Garden, and minor ones such as the Lyceum and the Olympic burnt to the ground but were rapidly rebuilt. In 1838, the Royal Exchange in the City was completely destroyed by fire. It was reported that the smoke and flames could be seen twenty-four miles from London. A new and grander building on an enlarged site was constructed. Six years passed before Queen Victoria formally opened the new Exchange.

The most dramatic fire of all was that of the Palace of Westminster. On the night of October 16, 1834, twelve fire engines and sixty-four men tried to put out a fire at the Palace of Westminster. Troops from the Brigade of Guards helped in working the fire engines but to no avail. Only the medieval Westminster Hall escaped destruction.

After the fire, Robert Smirke, architect at the Board of Works, and best known at that time for his work on the new British Museum, designed temporary accommodation for both the House of Lords and the House of Commons. The building work was completed by February 17, 1835. Work was soon underway on a new and more appropriate building, designed by Charles Barry and Augustus Welby Pugin. This was to be the largest public structure then built in London and took many years to construct. Finally, on April 15, 1847, Queen Victoria and Prince Albert opened the new House of Lords. The architecture and interior design were praised highly and described as 'the finest specimen of Gothic civil architecture in Europe'. The building was by no means finished and work proceeded on the construction of St Stephen's Tower, now better known as the Clock Tower. Preparations were made for installing the clock movement and the bells. In October 1857, the great bell, cast by Warner's at Stockton-on-Tees, cracked. It was recast at Mears's bell foundry in Whitechapel and the following year it was raised to the top of the tower. It later cracked again, hence the unique 'off-key' note of the bell we now call Big Ben.

During the second half of the nineteenth century many new landmarks appeared in the capital. They were, above all, symbols of progress. In Hyde Park, a spectacular international exhibition was held in 1851, displaying works of industry from all nations. No government money was spent on the project. To house the 100,000 exhibits, Joseph Paxton, the superintendent of the Duke of Devonshire's gardens at Chatsworth, designed a huge glass and iron structure. Using standardised components, it took only seven months to erect. The glaziers, working from specially-designed trolleys running along the roof, fitted over 300,000 panes of glass. It was named the Crystal Palace and became the most revolutionary building of the age. It was taken down after the exhibition and moved to Sydenham in South London. The profits of the Great Exhibition led to the creation of the South Kensington museum complex, as well as the Imperial Institute and the Royal Albert Hall.

London's new and extensive embankments revealed the Victorians at their most transformative. These ran on the north bank of the Thames in an almost unbroken line from Chelsea in the west to Blackfriars Bridge in the east and on the south bank from Lambeth Bridge to Westminster Bridge. The embankments were designed by Joseph Bazalgette, the chief engineer of the Metropolitan Board of Works, following the 'Great Stink' crisis of 1858 when the stench from the polluted river forced reconsideration of the capital's effluent disposal system. A long stretch of muddy foreshore was reclaimed for the Victoria Embankment and turned into a majestic roadway with gardens on one side and a riverside walk on the other. Beneath it, the new infrastructure of the city was set out with separate tunnels for the Underground, sewage and electric telegraph.

A VIEW OF WESTMINSTER ABBEY, C.1857

This photograph by Roger Fenton shows in the distance the scaffolding at the top of the Victoria Tower and the Clock Tower of the Palace of Westminster. This implies that construction work is nearing completion on London's new dramatic landmark. In the left foreground, the building site with a temporary wooden fence fronting Victoria Street reveals that more building work will shortly be underway. The ramshackle houses and walls opposite reveal something of the character and appearance of The Devil's Acre, a slum area located close to Westminster Abbey.

Previous page: **ALDGATE PUMP, 1880**

The Aldgate Pump marked the eastern edge of the City of London and was one of the capital's well known landmarks. Dickens, when writing about shabby-genteel people, refers to the pump at Aldgate along with the statue at Charing-Cross as examples of 'purely local' London things or characteristics.

LONDON STEREOSCOPIC AND PHOTOGRAPHIC COMPANY.

Above: **THE PALACE OF WESTMINSTER, c.1865**

This view from Lambeth shows the extent of the completed Houses of Parliament. Constructed from a combination of limestone and granite, the building covered an area of over three hectares.

Above left: **WESTMINSTER ABBEY, c.1865**

A new feature in front of the Abbey was Westminster School's Crimea Memorial, designed by Sir George Gilbert Scott. It was put up in 1861 in memory of the school's old boys who had lost their lives in this war and in India.

VIEW OF THE CLOCK TOWER FROM GREAT GEORGE STREET, c.1865

The Institution of Civil Engineers, now on the south side of Great George Street was on the opposite side when this photograph was taken, close to where the hackney coach is parked.

David Copperfield

'I have tamed that savage stenographic mystery. I make a respectable income by it. I am in high repute for my accomplishment in all pertaining to the art, and am joined with eleven others in reporting the debates in Parliament for a Morning Newspaper. Night after night, I record predictions that never come to pass, professions that are never fulfilled, explanations that are only meant to mystify. I wallow in words. Britannia, that unfortunate female, is always before me, like a trussed fowl: skewered through and through with office-pens, and bound hand and foot with red tape. I am sufficiently behind the scenes to know the worth of political life. I am quite an Infidel about it, and shall never be converted.'

WESTMINSTER HALL, 1860-70

This was the principal entrance into both the old and the new Houses of Parliament. Dickens would have known the old building inside out when he worked there as a parliamentary reporter. To serve the operation and function of government the old buildings had been converted and extended over the years. The arrangements were very inconvenient and to walk from one 'House' to the other one had to 'go down fourteen steps and come up seven'. Outside the entrance a cab rank was located ready to whisk away MPs and Lords after their sessions in the House had finished. Attached to and directly north of Westminster Hall were the Law Courts, housed in a Gothic style building that had been designed by John Soane. The edge of the structure can be seen in the left foreground of the lower photograph. The courts were relocated in 1882 when the new Royal Courts of Justice in the Strand were opened by Queen Victoria.

Excavation for the Metropolitan District Railway at Parliament Square and in Tothill Street by Westminster Abbey, c.1866

The statute of George Canning stands rather forlornly and precariously in an expanse of construction material and debris. The railway line was cut in this area over a six-week period and the contractor was subject to a penalty clause if the works were not completed on time. There were fears that landmark buildings such as Westminster Abbey would be damaged by the excavation and by the shaking of the railway engines and carriages. A layer of peat over two metres thick was packed along the south wall of the tunnel to reduce vibrations.

BUCKINGHAM PALACE FROM ST JAMES'S PARK, C.1890

The shallow lake of St James's Park, much larger in Victorian times than today, had pleasure boats for hire. The park extended almost to the railings of Buckingham Palace. The building was found to be unsuitable for Queen Victoria with a growing family and an active role in the affairs of state. In 1846 parliament voted £200,000 towards improvements and alterations. The most dramatic change was the addition of an East Front which hid Nash's classical façade and necessitated the removal of Marble Arch. The balcony on which the royal family appear today was added at this time. Queen Victoria first appeared on it, to the cheers of the crowd celebrating the opening of the Great Exhibition, in 1851.

BUCKINGHAM PALACE, C. 1857

Queen Victoria met Dickens once, at Buckingham Palace, on 9 March 1870. According to George Dolby they discussed 'the servant question' and 'the price of provisions, the cost of butchers' meat, and bread'. Despite having a painfully swollen foot he remained standing during the entire ninety-minute audience.

She found him 'very agreeable, with a pleasant voice and manner' and when he died later that year she noted that he was 'a very great loss. He had a large, loving mind and the strongest sympathy with the poorer classes'.

No. 493. General Post Office.

THE GENERAL POST OFFICE, 1865

St Martin's le Grand was a run down area of cramped buildings and narrow lanes, close to St Bartholomew's Hospital and the Smithfield live meat market. The building of the new General Post Office building was an attempt to improve the area. Over 130 houses were demolished and nearly 1,000 inhabitants had to move elsewhere. The building was designed by Sir Robert Smirke who was responsible also for the new British Museum. It was constructed in the dominant classical style. The inside and entrances to the building were lit by a thousand gas burners. Opened in 1829, the new General Post Office instantly became one of London's tourist attractions.

THE BRITISH MUSEUM, C.1860

On 8 February 1830 Charles Dickens, aged eighteen, obtained a reader's ticket for the British Museum, giving his address as 10 Norfolk Street, Fitzroy Square. He embarked on a course of miscellaneous literary and historical reading and some of his reader's slips requesting books have survived.

THE BANK OF ENGLAND, C.1860

This stereoscopic photograph shows the windowless Threadneedle Street façade of the Bank of England. Designed by John Soane, the interior space included numerous offices and committee rooms, nine open courts as well as a spacious rotunda that was completely hidden from the street.

VIEW FROM THE ROYAL EXCHANGE, C.1875

One of the busiest interchanges in London, with the meeting of seven streets, the hansom cabs and carts have become blurred as they are moving too quickly for the camera to freeze-frame their movement. The photograph is framed by the Mansion House on the left and the Bank of England on the right. It feels like a hot summer's day. However, one can make out drivers perched high up on heavily laden vehicles. In the foreground around the Duke of Wellington's statue there is a hive of activity. A shoeblack is polishing a man's shoes while other shoeblacks to the left are grouped in a circle, clearly deep in conversation. Further left, a woman stands next to a lamppost perhaps waiting to cross over Cornhill while a group of top-hatted businessmen to the right appear to be watching the traffic pass by. In the right foreground, two messenger boys are drinking from the fountain. Its bronze figure set above the granite base represents Temperance.

ROYAL EXCHANGE, c.1875

Looking east, with Threadneedle Street on the left and
Cornhill on the right, we are right at the heart of the
financial city. The impressive main façade of the Royal
Exchange with its Corinthian columns and classical
frieze lauding British commerce gives an impressive
aspect to the scene matched by Chantrey's fine
equestrian statue of the Duke of Wellington. A flower-
seller who rests her arm on one of the bollards and
carries a basket can be seen on the small central island
in the middle of road. Two omnibuses are picking up
passengers from in front of the Royal Exchange.

No. 468.—*The National Gallery.*

THE NATIONAL GALLERY, C.1865

The National Gallery, shown on the left, moved to its present site in Trafalgar Square in 1838. The Royal Academy was based there also until 1868. Dickens visited the annual exhibitions and in 1839 Daniel Maclise's portrait of him, known as the 'Nickleby' portrait, was displayed there.

TRAFALGAR SQUARE, LOOKING SOUTH-WEST, C.1857

Cabs wait in line for customers alongside Sir Francis Chantrey's statue of George IV. Facing them, but not visible in the photograph was Morley's Hotel, now the site of South Africa House. The base of Nelson's column is 'lion-less' as Landseer's sculptures were not installed until 1867.

VIEW OF TRAFALGAR SQUARE, C.1863

This stereoscopic card was sold at the time of the Royal wedding between the Prince of Wales (later Edward VII) and Princess Alexandra of Denmark. If held up to the light, it can be seen that the image has been pricked and coloured to celebrate the event and reflect the decorations in the streets.

MILLBANK PENITENTIARY, C.1865

This photograph shows one of the six panopticons of the prison. In the 1850s, it was London's largest prison and housed convicts from all over the country. Dickens describes the area to the west of Lambeth Bridge in *David Copperfield* as 'a dreary one at that time; as oppressive, sad, and solitary by night, as any about London. There were neither wharves nor houses on the melancholy waste of road near the great blank Prison. A sluggish ditch deposited its mud at the prison walls.' The prison closed in 1890 and was demolished soon after. The Tate Britain art gallery now stands on the site.

INNER COURTYARD OF NEWGATE PRISON, C.1895

Dickens devotes one of the *Sketches by Boz* to describing 'A Visit to Newgate'. He visits the condemned cells and describes the thoughts of a prisoner awaiting execution: 'Hours have glided by, and still he sits upon the same stone bench with folded arms, heedless alike of the fast decreasing time before him, and the urgent entreaties of the good man at his side. The feeble light is wasting gradually, and the deathlike stillness of the street without, broken only by the rumbling of some passing vehicle which echoes mournfully through the empty yards, warns him that the night is waning fast away. The deep bell of St. Paul's strikes – one! He heard it; it has roused him. Seven hours left! He paces the narrow limits of his cell with rapid strides, cold drops of terror starting on his forehead, and every muscle of his frame quivering with agony. Seven hours!'

Newgate Prison, c.1885

This view shows the north-west corner of the prison. Public executions which formerly took place at Tyburn, were transferred to Newgate in 1783 and took place in front of the prison until 1868. Vast crowds came to watch the spectacle. The prison closed in 1902 and was demolished shortly after.

NEWGATE 9x3 FGOS

CONSTRUCTION WORK ON THE VICTORIA EMBANKMENT, C.1869

This view shows part of the embankment to the west of Waterloo Bridge and at the foot of Savoy Street. The horse-drawn wagons were used to remove spoil from the site. This part of the Metropolitan District Railway line was constructed after the embankment had been built and proved more complex and costly than expected. The section between Westminster and Blackfriars opened on 30 May 1870 with grand opening of the Victoria Embankment slightly later on 13 July 1870.

A View of the Thames Embankment, c.1875

Looking east towards the City of London, the dramatic changes to the riverscape between Waterloo and Blackfriars Bridge are evident with the new wide tree-lined roadway running along the embankment. The single-storey building in the middle distance beyond Somerset House is the new Temple underground station. Charles Dickens admired the new scheme as he pointed out in a letter to a Swiss friend William de Cerjat in 1869, 'The Thames embankment is (faults of ugliness in detail, apart) the finest public work yet done. From Westminster Bridge to near Waterloo, it is now lighted up at night, and has a fine effect. They have begun to plant it with trees; and the footway (not the road) is already open to the Temple. Besides its beauty, and its usefulness in relieving the crowded streets, it will greatly quicken and deepen what is learnedly called "the scour" of the river.'

Chelsea Embankment looking east and west, c.1872

By the Victorian period, Chelsea was a densely populated suburb of London. In former times, it had been a quiet village, the home of the nobility and the wealthy. The Chelsea Embankment was the last of the three major Thames embankment schemes constructed by the Metropolitan Board of Works, under its chief engineer, Sir Joseph Bazalgette. On 9 May 1874, the Duke and Duchess of Edinburgh opened the embankment and part of the roadway. The view looking east shows the tower of Chelsea Old Church on the left and in the distance the unfinished Albert Bridge. In the photograph looking west, Cheyne Row on the right, once fronting directly on to the river, is now set well back from the Thames. In the distance part of the old Battersea Bridge can be seen which featured in James McNeill Whistler's controversial set of Nocturne paintings.

Little Dorrit

⌐∽⌐

'It was one of those summer evenings when there is no greater darkness than a long twilight. The vista of street and bridge was plain to see, and the sky was serene and beautiful. People stood and sat at their doors, playing with children and enjoying the evening; numbers were walking for air; the worry of the day had almost worried itself out, and few but themselves were hurried. As they crossed the bridge, the clear steeples of the many churches looked as if they had advanced out of the murk that usually enshrouded them, and come much nearer. The smoke that rose into the sky had lost its dingy hue and taken a brightness upon it. The beauties of the sunset had not faded from the long light films of cloud that lay at peace in the horizon. From a radiant centre, over the whole length and breadth of the tranquil firmament, great shoots of light streamed among the early stars, like signs of the blessed later covenant of peace and hope that changed the crown of thorns into a glory.'

PHOTOGRAPHER CREDITS

Atwood, William, 226, 246, 247, 248, 250, 251 (top); Bevington, Geoffrey 150, 151; Blanchard, Valentine 35(bottom), 40, 101, 136, 205, 220 (bottom), 260, 266, 272; Caldesi, Blandford & Co., 186 (top left); Claudet, Antoine, 190; Bool, A & J, 39, 41, 49, 50, 68, 69, 74, 76-77, 78, 79, 80-1, 138, 140, 204, 206, 207; Crace, J G, 28; Diamond, Hugh Welch, 180; Dixon, Henry, 1, 38, 42, 43, 44, 45, 46,47, 48, 51, 82, 83, 86,88, 89, 90, 93, 208, 209, 214, 215, 218, 219, 221; Downey, W & D 182 (bottom right); Edwards, Ernest, 182 (top right); Fenton, Roger, 2-3, 256, 265, 273 (top); Flather, Henry, 154, 156, 157, 158, 159, 160, 161, 162-3, 164-5, 166-7, 168-9, 170-1, 172, 174, 175, 262, 263, 278; Fox Talbot, William Henry 114, 115; Frith, Francis & Co. 264; Gawan, H, 251 (bottom); G R & Co, 259; Graphoscopic Company, 23; Heath & Beau, 184 (top right); Hedderley, James, 282, 283; Jones, Frederic 186 (bottom left);London Stereoscopic and Photographic Company Limited, 152, 153, 191, 258 (top); Maull & Polyblank, 189; Mayall, 182 (top left); Melhuish, A J 54-55; Melhuish & Haes, McLean 178; Morgan and Laing, 120, 121, 122, 123, 124, 126, 127; Petit, Pierre, 188 (bottom right); Sedgfield, Russell, 239, 241, 242, 243, 244, 245; Silvy, Camille, 184 (top left); Skeolan, Peter Paul, 185; Southwell Brothers, 186 (bottom right); St Croix, M, 26; Stratton, William Henry, 192, 193, 194, 195; Stuart, Francis G O, 33, 176, 276; Strudwick, William, 32, 57, 59, 60, 61, 62, 63, 65, 66, 67, 141, 196, 228, 234, 235, 253, 258 (bottom); Thomson, John, 58, 64, 71, 85, 94, 99, 100, 102, 103, 104,105, 106, 107, 108, 109, 110, 111, 131, 232, 233; United Association of Photography Limited, after Hugh Welch Diamond, 180; Unknown, 23, 24, 29, 30, 31, 34,3 5 (top), 36, 37, 52-53, 70, 73, 84, 95, 112, 116, 117, 118, 128, 130, 132, 134, 137, 143, 144-147, 148, 177, 201, 202, 203, 212, 213, 220 (top), 222, 223, 224, 236, 254, 261, 267 (top and bottom), 268, 270, 273 (bottom), 274, 275, 281; Valentine, James, 238; Watkins, George Herbert, 183; Watkins, John & Charles, 12, 188 (top left & right); Watkins, Octavius Charles, 181; Wilson, George Washington, 198, 210, 216, 230; York and Son, 98.

All images © Museum of London, except:
Pages 112, 118, 119, 120, 121, 122, 123, 124, 126, 127, 128, 130, 148 © PLA Collection/Museum of London
Page 26, © Victoria and Albert Museum, London.
Page 114, National Media Museum/SSPL
Pages 56, 59, 60, 61, 62, 63, 65, 66, 67, reproduced by kind permission of Lambeth Archives department

Prints of photographs from the Museum of London's collections that appear in this book may be purchased from www.museumoflondonprints.com

Note: page numbers in bold refer to information contained in caption titles.

ACKNOWLEDGEMENTS

Much thanks to Anna Sparham for tracking down photographs in the Museum of London's collection and to Claire Frankland for locating material in the port and river archive at the Museum of London Docklands; also to curators in the History Collections Department who have helped in the selection, dating and identification of photographs especially Beverley Cook, Hilary Davidson, Pat Hardy and Mike Seaborne; to Sean Waterman who managed the production of all the photographs, securing permissions and rights; to Torla Evans, John Chase and Richard Stroud, the Museum's photographers; to Sean O'Sullivan, the Museum's Head of Retailing who has supported the book at all stages; to Imogen Fortes and her team at Ebury Press; and finally to Peter Ward, the book's designer, who has set out the photographs, text and captions in a remarkable way.